DE
converted

Second Edition

a journey from religion to reason

Foreword by
Richard Dawkins

Seth Andrews

Author's note:

n this Second Edition of my autobiography, it's important to note
hat – obviously – my personal story hasn't changed, but ten years
)f activism and experience has helped me improve some of the lan-
;uage, most notably in Chapter 19-21, as I speak candidly about
itheist activism and offer some basic responses to common apolo-
;ist questions.

This Second Edition features a new Foreword from evolutionary
)iologist Richard Dawkins, and I've also updated the statistics for
The Thinking Atheist podcast and community. It has been an excit-
ng decade, and I'm so honored to be able to update "Deconverted"
'or a whole new audience.

Acknowledgements

Here at the beginning, I want to thank Natalie, the woman who has been my friend, advisor, conscience, theological sparring partner and the person who has colored my life with joy beyond words. Despite our differences, she has been a constant source of support, and through thick and thin, she continues to encourage me to be my true self, to speak honestly and to pursue the things I'm passionate about. Of the many successes I've had in these recent years, the happy home we've built together is the one I'm most proud of.

Despite our disagreements on religious issues, I owe a tremendous debt of gratitude to my mother and father for their love, their strength of conviction, and a genuine desire to see their children rescued from harm. We've had our moments of pronounced division, but even though my particular apple has fallen far from the tree, I have no doubt that our bond as a family can cross all barriers. The differences between us can now be the brands of individuality that make life all the more interesting, and it's my hope that my entire family will celebrate the desire of each child and grandchild to find his or her own voice.

The Thinking Atheist community was founded by a single person, but it has thrived because of the contributions of many volunteers and supporters. Their time, talents, wisdom, enthusiasm and passion have humbled me beyond words. To James, Meg, Marco, Hilary, William, Stacey, Thom and Gary, you make me look much better than I deserve, and I'm infinitely grateful for each of you.

I also must acknowledge those who have inspired me throughout my journey. Richard Dawkins was one of the first secular biologists I had ever been introduced to, and his books were a game changer during a critical time in my life. Jerry DeWitt brought the kind heart of a pastor into the often-harsh culture of non-belief. The work of former pastor Dan Barker has been hugely beneficial. Psychologist and sex educator Darrel Ray has helped me to blush a little less whenever my radio show explores issues of sexuality before an audience of thousands. James Randi encouraged me to embrace the doubts that once frightened me. Matt Dillahunty, AronRa, Faisal Saeed Al-Mutar, Cristina Rad, Evid3nc3, Sarah Haider, DarkMatter2525, Gayle Jordan, Anthony Magnabosco, NonStampCollector, Dale McGowan, Armin Navabi, and Andrew Seidel are among the activists who have impacted my work, and I've since connected with a new generation of atheist activists injecting new life into age-old religious discussions.

Perhaps the single most influential person in my journey was a man whose white-hot light was snuffed out far too soon. Christopher Hitchens rattled my cage, tickled my funny bone, and sent hurricane winds through the cobwebs between my ears. I often grieve that this treasure of a man is lost, and then I give thanks that I'm alive in an age where his books, his interviews, his speeches and his absolutely unique voice can be enjoyed and replayed for this generation and the ones to follow. I never had the opportunity to shake Hitchens' hand, but to my last day, I will consider him a friend.

Foreword

by Richard Dawkins

Imagine what it must be like to really believe there's a place called Hell, red hot and real, a post-mortem torture chamber of unspeakable horror where you will certainly, without any doubt, spend all eternity if you don't accept Jesus. I mean really, really, really believe it: believe it in the core of your being, believe it with as much total conviction as we all believe there's a place called the South Pole where it's very cold.

So, God is a petulant, vengeful sadist, then? A celestial narcissist so ignominiously vain that he'd spit-roast you for all eternity for the petty slight of not believing in him? Why would you credit anything so ridiculous? Really, really believe something so implausible? The reason is childishly simple. Literally childish. Your parents told you about it when you were a helpless child. Your beloved parents, your teachers and other respected adults, fed it to you when you were too young to know better: when you were vulnerable and gullble, credulous and trusting. That's all it takes.

Seth Andrews is spot-on right to call it psychological abuse: it is using the weapon of real, palpable terror, literally-believed terror, against children. But we should excuse the parents on the grounds that they themselves believe the very same nonsense with the utmost sincerity, and for exactly the same reason. Their own parents fed it to them. And so on back through the generations. And so it will go on forward, unless we find some way to break the tragic cycle and "save the children." To achieve that, we need lots more courageous breakaways like Seth Andrews.

Seth did more than break the cycle for himself. He is a gifted communicator, equipped to guide others out of the pit into which so many were thrown as children by well-meaning parents and grandparents, teachers and preachers. A charismatic broadcaster, podcaster and producer, this book shows him to be a gripping writer too. His is a great escape story, a lighthouse beam of hope for others. There's charm here too, not least in Seth's gentle sympathy towards his own parents. He's careful not to shame them. He doesn't blame them for stunting his education, shielding him from the glories of science and the true poetry of reality. Magnanimous, he forgives their thankfully failed attempt to impoverish his intellectual development and scare him witless with high Hadean threats. They meant well. They sincerely believed – still believe – that they must do all in their power to save him from the terrifying fate with which they in their turn were threatened by their own parents. What must it feel like to believe your much-loved son is hell bent on Hell and damnation? It is a horrible position they are in – one from which they themselves, and countless other loving parents in America's benighted bible belt, need rescuing.

Is it too much to hope (I fear it is) that parents like these will read Seth's book and repent? It's surely too much to hope they'll listen to me. Perhaps the fanatically religious Oliver Cromwell will strike a chord: "I beseech you, in the bowels of Christ, think it possible you may be mistaken."

h and, by the way, you actually are mistaken. Read Seth's book with
nything remotely approaching a receptive mind and you'll see why.

Richard Dawkins

Table of Contents

Introduction

"You were never really saved to begin with."

I hear this charge almost weekly. On my website. On YouTube. On Facebook. A passionate Christian reads my story and exclaims that nobody who'd experienced a legitimate encounter with the risen Savior could ever reject his love, his truth, and his gift of eternal life. I obviously wasn't ever a true believer. I missed a step. I did it wrong. Jesus never actually entered my heart. My religious upbringing, my salvation prayer, my baptism, my Bible-based education, my years as a Christian broadcaster, and my ultimate rejection of it all are null and void, because I had been a counterfeit.

Or perhaps I *had* once truly believed, but nearing my 40s, I simply lost my way. I'm going through a phase. I'm neck-deep in the throes of a midlife crisis. Family and friends might assert that, instead of the sports car and hair plugs, I've simply tried on a glamorous new worldview…something intentionally shocking and rebellious, brandished like a teenager's surprise tattoo at grandma's funeral, and they are probably convinced that, after a few years of sowing my wild oats (feeling all vigorous and sexy), surely I'll get it out of my system.

Living in this middle-aged skin, I can personally attest that there's nothing sexy about turning your life upside down at a time when some are considering early retirement. And unlike the flashy convertible, trendy haircut, or trophy spouse, this particular "phase" isn't simply laughed off, brushed off, or ignored.

Announcing you're an atheist is like drenching yourself in gasoline and showing up for a candlelight church service. The crowd is convinced you're going up in flames, and they're terrified that you'll take others with you. Some scatter. Some attempt to *cleanse* you. Some just stand there and scream, "Save the children!"

This does not make one feel young and vigorous. It's the stuff of wrinkles and ulcers and sleepless nights, made worse by the constant attempts by others to excuse it all away. *It's a fluke. You're deceived. You're ill. You're going through an angry time. It's a mid-life crisis!* The rationalizations are tossed at me constantly.

I do feel myself changing in tangible ways. A few unwelcome age spots stare back at me from the bathroom mirror. My voice, already deep, sounds like an old Volkswagon until I've had my coffee. I said goodbye to my 32-inch waist years ago. My forehead is crawling northward, mocking the full, lustrous hairs that have no doubt found a new home in the shower drain. I'm more practical. I'm less impulsive. I walk rather than run. I want my food richer. I want my music softer. I drive the speed limit. I'd rather have an hour-long massage than play Dance Party on X-Box. I watch and enjoy documentaries. I avoid spicy foods. I vacation at home. And I love to sleep.

Another side effect of getting older? When it comes to the ridiculous, the atrocious, and the insane, I've found that my fuse has gotten much, much shorter, and as I look at religion with fresh eyes, I n overwhelmed by public displays of the ridiculous, the atrocious, nd the insane. Wild mythology. Psychological abuse. Bad science. orruption. Blatant lies.

s a Christian for thirty years, I had long been an accessory to these rimes against education, science, and reason. For decades, I had ccepted without challenge the religious teachings of my family and ulture. I was the genuine article. I was a true believer. In August of 010, I did a radio interview with Dan Barker, a former evangelist nd current President of the Freedom From Religion Foundation. Vhen Dan said, "If I wasn't a true Christian, nobody is," I could otally relate. And now that I'm free, I've made it a life mission to xpose the flaws in the very teachings I once held so dear. For that eason, this book (and the majority of my work) focuses heavily on Christianity.

t has been a long, strange, painful, exhilarating, liberating, amaz- ng journey. And as I tell my own story, it is my sincerest hope that others might avoid the confusion, the frustration, and slow upward limb out of the stifling cocoon of indoctrination. It is also my hope hat those who've never seen religion from the inside will not be so quick to dismiss believers as hateful, bigoted, or mentally ill. I see hese stereotypes tossed out flippantly, and my personal experience as shown these accusations to be largely unfounded and untrue. Many, many religious people are good people. I simply assert that hey are good despite their superstitious beliefs, not because of them.

'm not a scientist. I'm not a philosopher. I'm not a former apologist or Bible scholar. I didn't graduate from an Ivy League university. 'm not a prodigy. I'm not a member of the intellectual elite. I'm ust an everyman, an ordinary person like billions of others, once loaked in the false security and flawed reasoning that inhibits so many in our world. Those looking for the erudition of Hitchens, Russell and Ingersoll will instead find a real-world story, told in plain English, of a young Christian man who climbed the ladder toward Heaven…and jumped.

None of what you're about to read is designed to shame or harm those in my inner circle. This book isn't a sensational exposé reeking of dirty laundry, nor does my family deserve such treatment. My mother, father, siblings, and extended family are beautiful people, and despite our disagreements, I remain a staunch advocate for their characters, their goodness, their love, and their Constitutionally protected right to worship as they see fit. I do claim my own right to examine and openly challenge the superstitions thrust upon me from birth, and I offer the sincere assertion that my end-goal is simply to find the truth. The few family-related details I include only serve to provide necessary context as I describe my own journey from Christianity to atheism.

You'll also see that I've prefaced each chapter with brief, personal statements submitted by the men and women of The Thinking Atheist online community. As their words have provided so much encouragement to me, I felt it was imperative to include a few quotes here to encourage others.

I often take heat for branding my website with the moniker, "The Thinking Atheist." Many say the title sounds lofty and arrogant. Some atheists call it redundant. The religious say it's an oxymoron. None of these are correct. The Thinking Atheist isn't a person. It's a symbol. The icon itself – a facial profile containing the atheist-A supernova - represents the rejection of faith and the embrace of reason. As Christopher Hitchens once said from the debate stage, "It's called faith because it's not knowledge," and he was exactly right. I don't want to simply believe. Whenever possible, I want to know for sure. And in those instances when I do not (or cannot) have an answer, I reject faith as the catch-all solution to the gaps in human understanding.

Wonderful things happen when you give yourself permission to acknowledge your doubts, to ask the hard questions, and to pursue the evidence wherever it leads. As my website's unofficial slogan says: **Assume nothing. Question everything. And start *thinking*.**

It sounds so simple. But as you'll see, it was nothing of the kind.

*"I know God exists, and he has
28 Twitter accounts to prove it."*

Rodrigo / El Salvador

CHAPTER 1
Train up a Child

The Age of Accountability. That's what they call it when a child is mature enough to become responsible for his own moral actions and eternal fate. The age varies, depending on the denomination, doctrine, and culture, but I distinctly remember sitting in the audience as a teenager on a Sunday morning in 1982 at Tulsa's Gracemont Baptist Church while children as young as 4 were paraded before the congregation to "profess their faith," because they were old enough to understand their own sin nature and accept Christ's gift of eternal life. They could comprehend the Jesus message. They understood who they were, what they were, and why they required rescue from their own unworthiness. They had reached the Age of Accountability.

Of course, most hadn't yet picked up a single elementary school textbook. They could sing the alphabet song, but they couldn't read with any real comprehension. They couldn't drive, drink, vote, or even watch certain television shows. Many hadn't graduated from tricycle to bicycle.

Theirs was the snot-nosed, sticky-fingered world of peanut butter sandwiches and cartoons, playgrounds and superhero pajamas, crayons and pop-up books, booster chairs and midday naps. Their world existed no farther than the reach of their tiny arms.

Yet they were somehow able to take personal and public responsibility for a hard-wired sin nature, implored to pledge allegiance to an invisible overlord they could not see, and charged to prevent their own torture in a nasty, horrible place that the Vacation Bible School teachers called Hell.

Looking back on my own early introduction to the fear of Hell, now see it as psychological abuse.

When I was a kid, the Sunday school messages consisted of little more than, "Yes, God made Hell. But he doesn't want you to go there. So accept Him, because he loves you." It was a clever little sleight of hand, where religious mentors excused Yahweh's chamber of horrors as a place he designed but didn't want to use. Hell was designated for the devil and his angels. Hell wasn't meant for us. And every time God was forced to send one of his lost children writhing and screaming into the inferno, it broke his heart. Yet God had no choice.

"Yes, God is love. But He is also just."

My parents were educated theologians. By teaching their children these things, they felt they were simply obeying God's command in Proverbs 22:6 to train up their child in the way that he should go. Anticipation of Heaven and fear of Hell were healthy. Natural. Normal.

When you're five and contemplating Hell, concepts like "proportionality" exist far out of reach, well beyond climbing range, unknowable. No young child can digest or discern whether such overt sadism is an appropriate punishment for the heinous act of simply being born as a descendent of Adam. The Adam and Eve story is resented so matter-of-factly inside the template of disobedience and punishment; it all just makes sense to a kid. In the Garden of Eden, God made a rule. Adam and Eve broke the rule. They were bad. God punished them. Now we are all bad. We all deserve punishment.

This made sense. This was my reality. And as far back as I can remember, I knew that I was a born a sinner. Unworthy. Undeserving. And I felt so very fortunate that Jesus came down from Heaven to save "a wretch like me," even though I had no idea what a wretch actually was. I knew it couldn't be good.

My parents treated the teachings of the bible as hard, concrete, indisputable fact. God was real. Satan was real. Adam sinned in the garden. Noah built an ark. Jesus was born in a manger, died on a cross, rose on the third day, and would someday return. Heaven and Hell awaited the dead. My whole life would be spent in thankful servitude for a gift I did not deserve. It was Stockholm Syndrome for kindergarteners.

For many, it's difficult to reconcile this kind of superstitious thinking with a secure and loving home life, but lest you conjure up crazy images of Westboro Baptist Church or the Branch Davidians, I must clearly state that my upbringing was the uneventful stuff of white, middle-class, Protestant America…the kind of environment you'd find in thousands of homes across the plains.

I'm one of six children and a fraternal twin, a mere five minutes younger than my counterpart, a sister. All of us were raised in a cocoon of love and security, our parents wholly dedicated to our care and genuinely eager to see each child grow into adulthood a well-rounded, happy (and Christian) adult.

Home was a safe zone, an inviting place filled with kindness, humor and (with most of the kids still living at home) constant activity. My mother and father fed the mouths, clothed the bodies, and doctored the skinned knees and broken bones of their accident-prone charges without hesitation, and there is zero doubt that either of them would have given their lives to protect us. They didn't resemble the stereotypical Bible-based patriarchy (actually, Mom was the alpha, which would have given the apostle Paul a fit!). Nor did they seal the walls shut, blocking out the secular world by forbidding amenities like television, pop radio, secular magazines and books, etc.

Certainly, my parents vetted the content of our shows-our comic books, our toys, our music, our clothing, etc, but we as kids didn' feel an overt alarmist tone in regard to those things. Mom wasn' walking the house with a magnifying glass looking for Evil, poised to rap us on the knuckles with a cane. No, this environment was relatively relaxed, and any concerns about inappropriate (worldly) influences in our lives were handled with even voices and relatively calm demeanors. Home was a good place, and my parents deserve tremendous credit for the love and security they provided in an atmosphere that was, in many respects, normal.

Don't get me wrong. It was a conservative home. It was a conservative *religious* home. Peppered throughout our genuinely happy and secure cocoon were striking, sometimes even alarming, Bible-based philosophies and teachings. Some were benign and even somewhat sensible. Others were not.

There was no swearing. "Darn" was even considered inappropriate, as it was obviously a substitute for the other d-word. "Heck" was equally frowned upon (I don't get the logic, either). Appropriate exclamations were limited to benign outbursts like, "Oh my goodness," as "Oh my God" was a direct violation of the 3rd Commandment. Looking back, I chuckle at the comical ways I used to avoid actually saying words I secretly knew would give me the most satisfaction. Darn! Shoot! Gosh! Gosh-DARN-it!!! I remember my grandfather's favorite zinger, "Feathers," which invariably elicited smiles as he vented frustration. It would be years before natural, adolescent rebellion would push my own rolodex of slang beyond a G-rating, and even now, my language never shades to blue in the vicinity of family.

Alcoholic beverages in the home? Absolutely not. Throughout my entire upbringing, there wasn't a single instance in which liquor was allowed in the house. Never a beer in the fridge. Hard liquor would have been doubly scandalous. After all, Ephesians 5:18 instructed the children of God, "And do not get drunk with wine, for that is debauchery, but be filled with the Spirit." My parents never imbibed, they refused to allow their children to even hum a beer jingle in jest, and we ultimately came to see the symbols of Budweiser, Coors, and Michelob to be the direct symptoms of ungodly living. Even today, if my parents saw a brew in my hand, I suspect they'd immediately plan an intervention.

Our childhood entertainment was tame, but still enjoyable. My sisters and I spent countless pre-teen hours with faces plastered to the television for shows like Gilligan's Island, The Andy Griffith Show, and the entire library of Warner Bros cartoons. I was weaned on classic Star Trek, Dr. Who, The Munsters, Super Friends and all things Jim Henson. On Saturday nights, we were even allowed to watch "The Love Boat," which now strikes me as bizarre, since the weekly characters on that show did more bed-hopping than the cast of "Animal House."

We were encouraged to read, and non-religious books weren't usually a problem, although they tended to fall along the lines of "Encyclopedia Brown" or other uncontroversial fare.

We seldom went to the movies. My father had a severe hearing impairment (later treated with the awe-inspiring technology of cochlear implants…SCIENCE!), so two-hour stints in a theater were difficult for him. The few films we did see were largely Disney affairs like "The Apple Dumpling Gang." PG movies were approached with suspicion, and the loathsome R-rated films were forbidden outright. (I was in 7th grade when I caught my first rated-R flick at a friend's house, the classic Blake Edwards sex romp "10." Of course, the film's clever script and adult-themed comedy went right over my head as I fell under the raw, naked, hormone-exploding spell of a young Bo Derek. Thank you, Cinemax.)

We were allowed to celebrate Halloween, with conditions. Costumes were fine, but my sisters and I weren't allowed to dress up as anything overtly dark or devilish. No demons, witches, warlocks, wizards, or vampires. Animals were fine. Ghosts were fine. Clowns were fine. Bible character costumes were especially fine. And every October 31st, we were allowed to ring the doorbells up and down our neighborhood street as we filled our bags with teeth-rotting delights.

Sex was a subject rarely addressed, and any reference to it was cloaked in a blanket of embarrassment and shame. Intimate activities portrayed on television were immediately turned off with barely a word. A photo of a scantily-clad magazine model would be duly snipped and trashed. Songs with suggestive lyrics were strictly policed. And even though my parents would occasionally mention the sanctity of sex as part of a God-ordained, marital union, sexuality was treated like unwelcome but unavoidable baggage that righteous people were charged to clumsily carry.

I completely understand the desire of my mother and father to shield their children from adult-themed content, and I'm not suggesting that 8-year-olds should have unfiltered access to sex-related material. I'm simply aware that we - as children in a deeply religious home - were never given the tools to properly understand natural attractions and behaviors, and as a result, we were often left to fend for ourselves in discovering what human sexuality was and how it worked.

The few tidbits of sex-related information that *were* taught in our religious upbringing were framed in the laughable-if-it-wasn't-so-sad context of the Christian Bible. According to Yahweh, homosexuality was a sin so heinous that it warranted the destruction of those who practiced it (ala Sodom and Gomorrah in Genesis 19). Adultery was something that could be committed, not just physically, but in the mind with the most fleeting of thoughts, as Matthew 5:28 declared: "But I say to you that whoever looks at a woman to lust for her has already committed adultery with her in his heart." Pastors and youth leaders taught sermons on the evils of lust, specifically in regard to masturbation. (To this day, some adults discourage teens from committing this heinous act of self-gratification with bizarre warnings about blindness or hairy palms.)

One of the worst examples was the Bible-based assertion that female sexual desire was actually a by-product of Eve's sin in the Garden of Eden, and as punishment, Eve's female descendents would be forever cursed. Genesis 3:16 declared, "Your desire will be for your husband, and he will rule over you." Adding insult to injury was the first portion of the same verse which informed all females that God "will greatly increase your pains in childbearing; with pain you will give birth to children."

What a tragic way to prepare young women for sexual maturity! Christianity had declared that sexual desire was tainted, merely part of a punishment meted out by a male deity, and that the inherited sin of an ancestor was responsible for the agony of childbirth. Sex wasn't a beautiful thing to be enjoyed by consenting adults. Sex was marred by disobedience, male dominance, and guilt, existing mostly as an obligatory act of procreation as humans obeyed God's command in Genesis 1:28 to "be fruitful and multiply."

Guilt would be the calling card of many such lessons. We were taught that Adam and Eve had ruined all of humankind, their original sin spreading like a cancer through the souls of billions, our only rescue coming from an entity we could not see, hear, smell, or touch. We were lost, but praise to Jesus, we had the opportunity to be saved.

I was nine years old when I said the salvation prayer at a revival service at Eastwood Baptist Church. (I later wondered why any healthy church would require revival, but the thought didn't occur to me on that occasion.) I don't recall much about that day. I don't even know the guest preacher's name. I just remember walking the aisle at the end of an emotionally charged fire-and-brimstone sermon, kneeling at the altar, fervently asking Jesus into my heart, and then standing in a line with half a dozen other freshly-rescued souls to profess our faith before the congregation. And as the pastor commended this young convert and announced news of my salvation, the audience nodded an approving "Amen."

Then I went home and said the exact same prayer again in my bedroom, just in case I left out something important and God didn't catch the omission. You can't be too careful.

I'd recite the salvation prayer every few years; fire insurance, in case the previous policies on my life had somehow expired. Repent. Renew. Receive. Rinse. Repeat. (I'm surprised at how common this is, as I've heard similar stories from website fans and forum users who went through their own attrition of repetition as children. The thought of so many young hearts burdened by feelings of unworthiness just makes me sad.)

I wasn't sad at the time, though. I felt liberated. I was free. I was washed clean, sanctified, redeemed by the blood of the Lamb (terms and phrases I'd heard from the Sunday hymnal). I'd been snatched out of the spindly clutches of Satan. And my parents couldn't have been prouder.

My, how times have changed.

"I am beyond frustrated that I was forced through the Catholic school system with no choices given to me."

-   Amy / Ontario, Canada

CHAPTER 2
Allegiance

I was in third grade at Carl Sandburg Elementary School when my parents started to hear some alarming things I'd picked up in homeroom class. I can't recall the specifics outside of one conversation where I explained to them what I'd learned about Neanderthal man, but my mother became concerned enough to pull her children out of secular education. By the end of summer, I was enrolled in the small, highly conservative, church-owned Temple Christian School.

TCS was a kind of biosphere- a small, self-contained campus mere blocks from Tulsa International Airport. I remember enjoying myself as a student there, but at the time, there was no way I could see this cocoon of insulation with any real perspective.

The dress code was the stuff of parody. Boys were required to wear red, white or blue slacks, a red, white or blue shirt, and a clip-on necktie peppered with tiny images of the American flag. Girls wore dresses in the same color schemes (no flags, though), walking the halls like patriotic paper dolls. Hair was almost uniformly parted, primped or curled for maximum properness, causing the bulk of the students and faculty to look like they had been time-warped in from the 1950s. Somehow, none of this seemed strange.

We played basketball in the church parking lot in our dress pants and shiny shoes. We prayed before opening our PACE lesson books and thanked Jesus for the sack lunches our parents had assembled the night before. Test papers required scripture "memory verses" right alongside questions about history, science, English and math. We attended weekly chapel services where, before the preacher's message, we saluted the American flag, the Christian flag, and the bible. I can still remember those pledges today, as they are seared into me after years of recitations:

I pledge allegiance to the Christian flag
And to the Savior for whose kingdom it stands
One Savior, crucified, risen and coming again
To give life and liberty to all who believe

Hands over hearts, not even cognizant of what we were pledging, dozens of students droned out verbal promises of allegiance to the symbols of our brainwashing.

I pledge allegiance to the Bible
God's Holy Word
I will make it a lamp unto my feet
And a light unto my path
And I will hide its words in my heart
that I might not sin against God

In retrospect, it all sounds very cultish. Rooms of impressionable minnows were programmed through repetition, surrounded by happy stories of scripture, but also subtly aware that a devil lurked in the darkness with designs on our very souls. These rituals were our reminders that we were required to pick a side and remain loyal to the end. As children, we had pledged an allegiance we were charged to carry through adulthood. We would grow up to be champions of righteousness, infusing positive, godly influence into our homes, relationships, workplaces, and government. Especially our government.

In fact, throughout my upbringing and education, I was often told how important it was for godly men and women to involve themselves in the political system, to vote, to support Christian candidates, to pursue positions of public influence, to rescue our country from the deadly jaws of secularism and proudly defend One Nation Under God.

We were taught that America was a Christian nation, forged by Founding Fathers deified as saints in our (wildly incorrect) religious history books. God had cast the United States in a mold long since twisted by the influences of Satan. We were the next generation charged to retake the high ground and defend America's spiritual roots.

My grooming for battle was temporarily halted after a snit between my mother and the TCS principal over some since-forgotten issue, and I was yanked mid-year to finish the 4th grade via home schooling. I've since come to see many religious home school environments as cocoons even more restrictive and destructive than entities like TCS, as children are so often inhibited intellectually, emotionally, and socially by the parents/teachers eager to protect them from the big bad world. Certainly, there are exceptions, and I'm not an opponent of home schools, as I feel they can provide great benefit *in the correct circumstances*. My own short tenure in home school was uneventful, just a way to finish out the year.

In the fall of 1978, I attended my first class at Eastwood Baptist

Elementary, a far different animal than TCS and a much better fit. Eastwood would be my school home for seven years, providing the backdrop for some wonderful, cherished memories. I met my best friend of twenty-five years at Eastwood, and we remain close today. I sang bass in the choir and held major roles in the school productions of "The Music Man, "Fiddler on the Roof," and "Oklahoma." I joined the rowdy football fans on clunky yellow buses and cheered the team on until my voice gave out. I was a natural leader, ultimately becoming student council president my senior year.

My grades weren't stellar. Average. I certainly wasn't valedictorian material, preferring instead to skim by with so-so scores and enjoy the more social aspects of school. Ironically, I was disinterested in history and science, preferring to put my efforts into math and English. Especially English. It was during this time that I developed my love for language and began to hone the communication skills that would one day serve me as a broadcaster.

By my freshman year, I was commonly on-stage making presentations, emceeing events, and representing my school as a spokesperson for Youth for Christ. I vividly remember speaking on behalf of YFC at a fundraising banquet when the not-yet-Governor of Oklahoma Frank Keating came up to my mother and proudly exclaimed, "That boy has finesse!"

Finesse? I had to go home and look it up.

It seemed I was becoming the kind of positive Christian influence my parents and teachers had hoped for. But none of this felt forced or inappropriate. I was allowed to be a teenager, to date, to go to the movies, to involve myself in the secular culture. My school seemed like a healthy reflection of what real Christianity was all about. We felt like we lived in and mingled with the real world.

Eastwood bucked the private school stereotype, eschewing stuffy uniforms for blue jeans and t-shirts, our only dress-up day being chapel Wednesday (a common denominator in Christian schools). The atmosphere was relaxed and positive. Our music, drama and sports teams interacted and competed with those at public institutions. We actually felt somewhat like a regular school, the major differences being a slightly stricter dress code (teachers would measure the girls' skirt length with military precision), prayer before classes, an actual Bible class, and the aforementioned mid-week chapel service.

It was at one of these services that I would be introduced to a disturbing series of independent Christian films that would inject a stunning, sobering darkness into all of the happy Jesus talk and baptize me into the bloody, tumultuous, terrifying waters of the book of Revelation.

"I was 8 years old in Sunday school being told about Hell and why I should avoid it at all costs, because if you go there you will burn for eternity and suffer unending torture."

- **Michael / Marietta, Georgia**

CHAPTER 3
Scared Straight

The film was called, "A Thief in the Night," a 1972 shot-on-a-shoe-string depiction of the Second Coming of Christ. I was in junior high when my Christian school held a special screening for the entire student body. Produced by an obscure, independent film company, Mark IV Pictures, for $60,000 and cast with unknowns, this movie nonetheless shook me to my core.

Apologists snipe at each other over the details of Christ's return, but the essential premise of the Rapture goes like this: At any moment, Jesus will fulfill his promise in Matthew 16:27 to "come in his Father's glory with his angels," drawing all Christians from this earth into Heaven to join him and receive their eternal reward.

1 Corinthians 15:51-52 says, "Listen, I tell you a mystery: We will not all sleep, but we will all be changed—in a flash, in the twinkling of an eye, at the last trumpet. For the trumpet will sound, the dead will be raised imperishable, and we will be changed."

"A Thief in the Night" portrayed the Rapture scenario with grainy, 70s-era sepia tones, cheap sets, and an eerie synth soundtrack, the film's characters sporting bell bottoms and handlebar moustaches. Those browsing YouTube today for clips will probably guffaw at this dated, ham-handed attempt at high drama, but as a pre-teen, I remember the snickers quickly giving way to genuine, bone-chilling fear.

In the film version of the Christ's second coming, there was no actual trumpet. No fanfare. No splitting of the skies and grand announcement from the heavens. Jesus himself was never seen or heard. Instead, on a nondescript weekday morning, without warning, billions of people simply vanished.

"A Thief in the Night" opened with the ticking of a clock and the sound of a radio newscast announcing a sudden mass disappearance. A frantic wife called out through the house for her husband, the only trace of him being a still-buzzing electric razor lying in the sink. The implication was that the Christian husband had been snatched away to Heaven, leaving his unsaved wife behind to endure the Tribulation.

If Hell is the first-strike weapon that religious fear pimps use to frighten lost souls into salvation, the story of the Tribulation is the second-wave assault. The Tribulation is the post-Rapture period where Christ abandons the world completely, removing any and all protection, intervention, and communication. Satan assumes control of the earth for seven years, and chaos reigns.

Again, you can put fifty Bible experts in a locked room, and no two will agree completely on the Tribulation scenario. But for the purposes of the film, the seven-year Tribulation came immediately after all Christians were raptured away, and the poor unsaved people who remained were caught in a meat grinder of persecution, oppression, and terror.

As an impressionable young kid reared by theologian parents, I was already primed to receive these wild scenarios as truth. I'd been softened up by years of mealtime prayers, Sunday school lessons, and memory verses.

So you can imagine my alarm as "A Thief in the Night" (and the sequel films shown to us in succession) depicted an oppressive, military-style round-up of the populace to be permanently tattooed with the number of the beast, 666, a symbol which announced submission to the Antichrist and assimilation into an evil New World Order branded by a single word, "Unite."

The film series depicted the incarceration and execution (by guillotine) of those post-rapture converts who pledged allegiance to God. Many who had seen the light too late and missed the Rapture ultimately came to their senses and accepted Christ, only to have their heads chopped off in a public square. I still remember the bloody images of severed heads carried off in baskets. Carnage.

The films employed many familiar movie elements– car chases, soundtrack stings, monsters (yes, monsters) - yet the action was posited as something that would inevitably happen. These unbelievable, horrible, catastrophic scenarios would become our reality if we didn't drop to our knees and allow Jesus to rescue us. This message was reinforced in the film's theme song by Larry Norman, "I Wish We'd All Been Ready":

A man and wife asleep in bed
She hears a noise and turns her head, he's gone
I wish we'd all been ready.

Two men walking up a hill
One disappears and one's left standing still
I wish we'd all been ready.

There's no time to change your mind
The Son has come and you've been left behind.

When the credits rolled on "A Thief in the Night" and the lights came up, the school chaplain gave an invitation, asking if anyone wanted to come forward to accept Jesus Christ as personal savior. A mass of teary-eyed teenagers rushed the altar, desperate to escape their impending doom, crying out for God to save them before it was too late.

The memory sickens me.

Well-meaning parents, teachers, and counselors had attempted to scare the literal Hell out of impressionable children. And by using the tactics of terror to sell eternal salvation, they had no doubt scarred the very minds and hearts they were trying to protect.

These films weren't about the tangible benevolence of a loving Father. They didn't provide any proofs of God's existence or the Truth of scripture.

Instead, they employed shock and awe, blood and barbarism, paranoia and pain. They were a disorienting ride through Hades' House of Horrors. And by stamping the imprint of fear onto our hearts, these films (in my opinion) did great damage to thousands of young people programmed to feel inadequate, unworthy, vulnerable, persecuted, and afraid of the future.

Fear is a powerful weapon. It keeps us in submission. It stops us from asking too many questions. And as I grew from student to adult in the years ahead, fear would mute my own innate curiosity and concerns about the foundation my life had been built on. I would be continually told how much God loved me, but the underlying threat of the Tribulation and Hell would keep me in lockstep with the rest of my religious family, friends, and culture.

One day the Son would come. And I didn't want to get left behind.

"The most frustrating thing for me was being told lies by people I trust."

-   **Samantha / Auckland, New Zealand**

CHAPTER 4
Rock For The King

My teenage years coincided with the emergence of a genre of music that would ultimately attract millions of religious fans and draw the condemnation of pulpit-pounding conservatives across the nation. Spearheaded by the popularity of a fresh faced 16-year-old named Amy Grant, this edgier flavor of gospel called Contemporary Christian Music (CCM) would blossom from basement studios and shoestring budgets to become one of the fastest growing formats on the American music scene.

In the 70s and 80s, I frequented the local Christian bookstores for the few artists that were available: The Imperials. The Sweet Comfort Band. David Meece. A handful of others. There were harder groups like The Resurrection Band that appealed to the rock/metal crowd, but their albums were stacked right alongside tamer counterparts mere feet from a litany of other Christian-themed merchandise: bibles, Sunday school supplies, religious art, inspirational calendars, motivational books, and cross necklaces.

Many traditional (aka: older) Christians despised this new brand of gospel music, which stood in stark contrast to the three-piece suits and folksy melodies that reflected their own muted lifestyles. I remember hearing a revival preacher froth and wail over the evil influence of one particular CCM band, Petra, warning about the slippery slope of decadent living that would no doubt result from this wild mix of guitar solos and sexual rhythms. This particular preacher decried the downfall of America's innocence, apparently unconcerned about the country music he personally adored. Slow dancin', beer drinkin' and down-and-dirty lovin' were fine, but those rocky riffs and drum solos were the devil's playground. (Throughout my life, I've often been amused by how preachers' condemnation of pop culture fads as "evil" so often reflects their own personal tastes.)

In the 80s and early 90s, the quality of Contemporary Christian Music was almost universally poor, but there was a real affection for these artists and bands throughout the religious community. I was a huge fan, spending copious amounts of allowance money as the cassette cases stacked up on my bedroom shelves. I memorized the lyrics. I knew the biographies. I attended the concerts (often standing in long lines for primo seats). And I refused to taint myself with the bad influences of "secular" music, taking tremendous pride in committing myself to the godly alternative.

We fans felt waves of coolness fall upon us as we baptized ourselves in guitar solos, double-bass drum riffs, pyrotechnics, and glowing neon crosses descending onto smoke-covered concert stages. The poster child for this facepalm-worthy spectacle was the band "Stryper," a wall-of-sound Christian metal band adorned in yellow and black stripes, fronted by a guy whose car-alarm vibrato was high enough to shatter glass. And as the guitars crunched and the drummer's hair flailed with every strike of the snare, lead singer Michael Sweet would wail through ½ inch of cake make-up to implore God's messengers, "Loud and clear! Let the people hear!!!"

If I may reference the famous Rob Reiner mocumentary, this was Spinal Tap.

But I was hooked. And as a relatively sheltered teenager enjoying the idea that I was able to air guitar for Jesus while my schoolmates sold out to Satan, I made the music of Michael W. Smith, DeGarmo & Key, Servant, Petra, Margaret Becker, Rez Band, Shelia Walsh, and Russ Taff the soundtrack of my life. I rarely settled for less than 10th row seating at concerts. I wore the t-shirts. I hung the posters. I subjected the poor, trapped passengers in my car to the songs I felt might best draw them away from "devil music."

Of course, almost everything in my cassette player was CCM's attempt to copy what was popular in the mainstream. Leslie Phillips was our Stevie Nicks. Kathy Trocolli was our Taylor Dayne. Phil Driscoll was our Joe Cocker. Sheila Walsh was our Sheena Easton. Phil Keaggy was our Paul McCartney.

And the Christian rock bands also took their cues from the secular superstars that dominated popular music at the time. Do a Google search of 1980s Christian album covers, and you'll see the big-haired, spandex-adorned, makeup-wearing copycats of bands like Def Leppard, Poison, Motley Crue and countless others, all shaking fists in the air and belting out holy anthems like "Rock For The King" and "To Hell With The Devil."

A prime example of CCM's plagiaristic tendencies came on the heels of "We Are The World," a feed-the-hungry charity effort which combined legends like Michael Jackson, Luther Vandross, Bruce Springsteen, Tina Turner, Billy Joel, Steve Perry, and Diana Ross singing side-by-side. With sales of over 20 million, "We Are The World" was a landmark relief effort, raising over $10 million for USA For Africa in four months.[1]

Meanwhile, Contemporary Christian Music stood shell-shocked and embarrassed that the non-religious community had been at the forefront of a "missions" effort that should have been spearheaded by actual missionaries. CCM soon attempted its own version of the multi-artist anthem, a bland and uncomfortable rip-off called "Do Something Now," but every time the radio played it, there could be no doubt that it was as much an attempt to save face as it was a famine-relief anthem. The song released, played for a short run on Christian radio, and disappeared.

Image would become more and more important to the Christian recording industry in the years ahead. Personally, I was enjoying the image of student leader, role model, and positive influence, and CCM provided the soundtrack for this persona.

As I look back at it, I was the kind of guy that Christian parents adored and their children merely tolerated. For my classmates, the Mr. Clean routine must have kept me from being invited to more than a few parties. I never smoked. Never drank. Never experimented. And even my dating relationships remained relatively benign until I'd graduated from high school. I was the ultimate non-threat. I was the Nice Young Man.

At sixteen, I even played keyboard for a Christian band called "Corban," our moniker found in some obscure Bible dictionary, translating "sacrifice to God." I had big dreams, listening to my favorite Christian groups and cultivating my own aspirations to keyboard-solo for the King. Corban played parties, talent shows,

---

1   Glave, Judie (May 17, 1985). "USA for Africa readies for first mercy mission". *The Gainesville Sun*. July 21, 2009.

youth functions, even a skating rink. We weren't even small-time. We went nowhere. In retrospect, it's not difficult to understand why. We sucked.

But while Corban ultimately waned and disbanded like a million other garage warriors, my love for Christian music became only more intense. By the time I graduated high school, I had almost no idea what songs populated the Billboard Top 20, but I could report the Contemporary Christian Top 10 from memory.

I didn't realize it at the time, but this passion for CCM would soon translate into my first radio job, ultimately propelling me to the lead on-air position at one of the top Christian stations in the United States.

Mr. Clean was going public.

*"We can only move forward if
we can question our own beliefs."*

- **Jason / Northern Ireland**

CHAPTER 5
The Rise of Religion Radio

In 1990, KXOJ 100.9FM was a blip on the map…a radio station hardly anyone knew and even fewer cared about.

I'd listened to KXOJ in the 80s, and it had been a love/hate relationship from the start. My affection for the CCM format was strong, but the KXOJ radio announcers were almost uniformly awful. Their wattage was 1/10th of their corporate-owned competitors. Their commercial breaks sounded like something you'd hear after the 4:00 a.m. farm reports in a small hick town. They aired half-hour programs from radio evangelists who would spend twenty minutes screaming Bible verses and the final ten begging for financial "ministry partners." And ultimately, they couldn't compete with the power and polish of the better-funded, tamer, more conservative, more mainstream Christian powerhouse KCFO 98.5FM, "The Love Station."

KCFO had better music, better announcers, and better promotions. They were polished and professional. Sure, they played lots of commercials, but they never begged for money.

Begging would be a staple of KXOJ. Between 6:00 p.m. and 6:00 a.m. every day, once an hour, a commercial-free show called "The Gospel According To Music" (G.A.M.) would hit the brakes to plead for donations: 12 times a day. 84 times a week. 4,300 times a year. Hour after hour, the announcer would let the song end, take a deep breath and spend five ear-numbing minutes explaining that KXOJ was on a mission to change lives for Jesus, that commercial-free radio meant the listeners would have to pony up the thousands of dollars for monthly operating expenses, and that God would bless their generous gifts.

My friends and I hated this. I remember wishing KXOJ would have a little dignity and just play some damn commercials. I had no idea that, in 1990, my first-ever radio job would have me sitting behind the microphone as host for G.A.M, shilling for donations like the snake oil salesman I promised I would never become. Twelve-hour overnight shifts were common at KXOJ, and my first day on the air was just such a marathon. I'd gotten the job after taking broadcasting classes and putting together some roughshod demo tapes, calling around to different radio stations looking for a way into the business. I had no experience outside of mock radio shows recorded in classrooms and graded by teachers. I had nothing to offer except a deep voice, the enthusiasm of youth, and zero pride.

This attitude would help me survive some tumultuous months at KXOJ. The owner was a volatile man almost universally disliked by the on-air announcers, and kowtowing in fear of the next angry outburst became a shared experience we would only whisper about.

The physical environment only added to the feeling that I'd slipped into some kind of parallel universe. The studio building was located in a small pasture just off of I-44, and it wasn't uncommon to be on-air reading liners about upcoming contests while the reflections of cow faces stared back through the glass. The boss kept mousetraps in the transmitter room adjacent to the main studio, and the winter months were filled with the SNAPS and summary executions of field mice which had crawled into the equipment to get warm. Other creatures would sneak into the building at random. Snakes. Insects. And on one unfortunate occasion, a scorpion, which fell from the ceiling onto the main sound board during the 11:45 p.m. on-air prayer time. (I froze in terror until it crawled off. The listeners never knew a thing. Perhaps they thought it was a move of the Holy Spirit.)

There was a certain charm to some of this. Yes, I made pennies and worked in a shack among the weeds, but I was a real, professional radio announcer. I'd found a niche I could actually fill, and I was working a musical playlist I already knew by heart. The few listeners we had were kind and extremely supportive, as if they realized that we were the underdog in a David & Goliath struggle against the big boys. They forgave our many shortcomings and rooted for us to blossom into something much bigger and better.

In 1988, our powerhouse competitor KCFO sold out, and its new owners switched 98.5FM to a country music format. KCFO fans were livid. But KXOJ had been waiting in the wings for just such an opportunity. This tiny shack in the weeds was suddenly Tulsa's only option for Contemporary Christian Music radio.

By 1992, I had graduated from overnight shift to morning drive. I'd like to say it was because I was a kick-ass radio announcer, but the truth is much less glamorous. I'd simply avoided the revolving door and outlasted other DJs that had either been fired or found other jobs. Turnover at KXOJ (and in most radio stations, to be fair) was high, so the key to advancement was to simply stick around. Work the shifts. Develop a relationship with the audience. Do the grunt work. Stay visible. Just hang in there.

My tenacity paid off. I got promoted. I was now doing a radio show for a whole new audience. I was The Morning Guy. I was king of a very small anthill. The pay wasn't much better, but the new time slot freed me from the nightly beg-a-thons and allowed me a normal sleep schedule. Things were looking up. The sun was rising on me (and on the neighboring cows) every weekday morning from six to ten.

And then something crazy happened. In the mid 90s, Contemporary Christian Music - the poster child for bargain-basement production values and mom-and-pop religious bookstores - got popular.

Amy Grant's 1985 crossover hit "Find A Way" paved the way for her 1991 smash, "Baby Baby," waking audiences and record execs from their sleep and introducing them to this new, tamer, cleaner, family-friendly alternative to secular pop music.

While early 90s pop stations peppered young teenagers with (for the time) increasingly suggestive songs like Prince's "Cream" and Color Me Badd's "I Wanna Sex You Up," the marketplace was ripe for a brand of radio that required no warning labels, no parental supervision, no restrictions, no apologies. And CCM was waiting in the wings to fill that gap. The industry motto could have been, "Our artists don't drink, smoke, snort, shoot up, swear, or fornicate." (My next chapter reveals how this couldn't have been further from the truth.)

Music industry powerhouses had already swooped in and begun to take over. Boutique operations like Myrrh, Benson, Reunion, Maranatha, Star Song, Sparrow, Dayspring, and others were acquired by goliaths like Warner Music Group, EMI, Sony, Columbia and RCA. And with those acquisitions came increased budgets, fancier recording studios, name-brand producers, better marketing, and a larger footprint for Christian music in the marketplace.

In previous years, mainstream retail outlets' Gospel music sections were either an afterthought or non-existent. But by the mid-90s, it became common to see major mainstream retailers feature a Contemporary Christian category in their music departments, displaying the latest CDs from Amy Grant and 4 Him just a few rows down from Aerosmith, Celine Dion, Usher, and the Goo Goo Dolls.

Religious music had gone mainstream. Christian pop songs became slicker and catchier. The album covers became less amateurish, more polished. The artists got prettier (or at least had better airbrushing). The concerts got bigger and flashier. The videos...well...the videos still sucked. But still, Christian music fans found themselves apologizing less and less for the genre they loved.

By the year 2000, Contemporary Christian Music had blossomed into a $450 million industry in the United States, with SoundScan reporting 50 million units sold the previous year...more than jazz, classical and new age combined.[2] People across America were responding to songs about God, Jesus, faith, and family. I even had some non-believers admit they'd scanned the radio and hummed the music for days before realizing they'd been "tricked" into enjoying something religious.

And KXOJ had ridden this surge, hiring better announcers, eliminating the begging and preaching, buying a station van, using national-level jingles, doubling its wattage, and graduating from the obscure shack in Sapulpa, Oklahoma to a slick new studio on the 59th floor of Tulsa's Cityplex Towers.

And as KXOJ climbed from obscurity to become one of the most successful CCM radio stations in the country, I had a front row seat

---

2   Frank Breeden, CEO Gospel Music Assoc. CNN 12-14-2000

in the morning show chair.

I'd gained a co-host in 1994. Jim Marbles (yes, Marbles) was a goofy, hysterically-funny radio veteran who was actually more qual ified for my job than I was. He'd done mainstream radio work foi many years. He had the name recognition and honed talent that I dic not. Yet he patiently put up with this green, immature, inexperiencec minnow as I learned how "real" radio worked and developed my own signature style. He was my mentor, and I owe more to his inpu and influence than I can possibly express.

We became a Martin/Lewis team. I was the straight man. Marbles was the mischievous ham. I was disorganized and confrontational. He was meticulous and passive. We were polar opposites, on-air and in oui personal lives. But there was an immediate chemistry. We clicked. And by the late 90s, "Seth & Marbles in the Morning" grew to become Tulsa's #2 morning show in our target audience of adult females. We were recognized wherever we went. We appeared on television. We hosted charity events. We emceed major concerts. We had cardboard likenesses of ourselves displayed at retail stores. "Seth & Marbles" and KXOJ became recognizable local brands, our programming ev- ery bit as professional as our non-religious counterparts.

Radio listeners became family. Even now, my remembrances of the relationships I developed at KXOJ bring a smile to my face (and an ache to my gut). These Christian men, women, and children on the other side of the dial were not the caricatures of dangerous ig- norance drawn so often by the atheist community. They weren't mouth-breathing hicks. They weren't uneducated slobs. They weren't drones, cult members, fanatics, or freaks. They were beauti- ful, happy, compassionate, intelligent and enthusiastic. They greeted us with warm handshakes and hugs. They wore contagious smiles.

And just like the non-religious community, their days were a difficult, real-world balancing act of careers, families, goals, hobbies, passions, challenges, questions, heartbreaks and triumphs.

They were real, relatable people. They were good people. They were my friends.

But as I connected with this growing throng of listeners and fans, my radio family (and my real family) remained blissfully unaware of my own struggles against a growing cynicism and skepticism, an uncomfortable splinter of doubt just beneath the skin that was becoming more difficult to ignore.

"In the back of my mind I think I always had problems with the contradictory notions that God represented. I studied apologetics, led adult bible studies, served on church committees and tried to talk myself into rationalizing things. Perhaps, if I said it often enough, I'd really come to believe it."

- Allen / Austin, Texas

CHAPTER 6
Mysterious Ways

Doubt is a funny thing. It nips at you. It whispers to you. It's the subtle rapping inside your own skull. It's the gentle nudge forward or backward. It amplifies the obvious. It attempts to reveal the covert. And if we'd only stop for a moment to listen, we might in our own lives observe the wisdom in the words of Rene Descartes, "If you would be a real seeker after truth, it is necessary that at least once in your life you doubt, as far as possible, all things."

But doubt is messy. Doubt is inconvenient. And I had become adept at brushing away my doubts, even though the red flags waved at full mast in my personal and professional life.

One huge example. Our new KXOJ studios were located high atop the Cityplex Towers. Many know the Cityplex by its former name, the City of Faith Medical and Research Center, a facility commissioned by evangelist Oral Roberts and cloaked in controversy after he'd announced in 1980 that he had seen a vision of Jesus as tall as a skyscraper. Roberts proclaimed, "When I opened my eyes, there He stood, some 900 feet tall, looking at me; His eyes, oh, his eyes! He stood a full 300 feet taller than the 600 foot tall City of Faith".[3]

---

3   Tulsa World Oct 6, 1980

The faithful applauded this vision as miraculous. Skeptics decried it as the tall tale of a charlatan. Late night comedians roasted Oral Roberts over an open flame. Debate raged inside and outside of church circles as to the legitimacy of this grand escapade. (I remember quietly wondering why an evangelist who conducted worldwide *healing* crusades would need a hospital. Couldn't he erect a tent and call in the miracles?)

Despite the controversy, the City of Faith opened in 1981- a gaudy, three-tower monstrosity adorned in gold mirrors and featuring a 648-foot center structure, the second tallest building in Oklahoma.

Shortly after its grand opening, the City of Faith Medical and Research Center, built with divine direction under God's command, was largely vacant and drowning in debt. Time magazine reported annual deficits of over $10 million by 1986.[4]The fanfare, ribbon-cutting, confetti and shouts of praise had given way to the real-world challenges of supporting and maintaining a high-dollar medical facility. (God had apparently used up his mojo on the 900-foot Jesus effigy and couldn't be bothered to keep his own hospital solvent.)

So, in 1987, you can imagine the howls of disbelief and disgust from critics when Oral Roberts announced that he'd had yet another vision. God had appeared to him on a January day and commissioned him to raise $8 million for cancer research by March. Failure to reach this 90-day goal would be met with a strict penalty. Oral Roberts would die. God would "call him home."

I'll admit it. Morbid curiosity made me secretly want to see the goal unreached, but benefactors crawled out of the woodwork, copious amounts of cash were donated, Oral Roberts escaped the holy

---

4   http://www.time.com/time/magazine/article/0,9171,964970,00.html

hangman's noose, and the City of Faith was again hailed as a world hub for cutting-edge cancer research and medical care.

Yet only two years later, the City of Faith finally succumbed to a $25 million debt, closed the hospital, and converted to office space under its new moniker, the Cityplex Towers.

The irony? KXOJ's new broadcast studio was soon perched on the 59th floor of god's ghost town, a facility conceived with prayers, praises, and prophecies before being abandoned by the very ones who had deemed it so necessary, so divine, so ordained, so critical. It had become the City of Failure.

Largely in disrepair and modestly occupied, the Cityplex Towers loomed like a rusty totem over the campus of Oral Roberts University, a constant reminder of unkept promises and unrealized miracles. When KXOJ signed its lease in 1994, the facility was largely in disrepair. The lobby escalators were shut down, the fitness center was an empty warehouse, the atrium was a dusty shell, and the long hallways betrayed rows of doors leading to unoccupied spaces once earmarked for great things. The building had a pulse, but it was on life support with a new identity.

In the following years, whenever I'd hear someone talk about how God opened the doors for KXOJ to enjoy these newer, fancier ac- commodations, I'd have to swat away the incessant, annoying whis- per of doubt which was asking why the omniscient, omnipotent God of the universe couldn't successfully manage a hospital.

A common explanation by the faithful? The Lord works in mysteri- ous ways.

Of course, Oral Roberts' credibility had always been the subject of rabid debate within the Christian community, the naysayers claiming that the City of Faith wasn't God's failure, because it was never truly God's idea to begin with. (No word on why God wouldn't step in and prevent a false prophet from misrepresenting him to the entire planet.

For me, this excuse highlighted a tactic within the church to "count the hits and ignore the misses." If something amazing or wonderful transpired, it was God in action. If something terrible happened, it was man's fault or the handiwork of Satan, and God was given a pass.

Get a hefty raise at the office? Thank God. Get fired from your job? Blame the devil, or merely assert that God had closed a door so that he could open a window. Convenient.

And the devil must've had his hands busy, because I saw evidence of his sinister deeds everywhere. Tragedy struck Christian men women and children every day. Hand-picked, beloved, protected Children of The Living God were maimed in accidents, riddled with sickness, "afflicted" with alcoholism, drug use, teen pregnancy, domestic abuse, bankruptcy and all manner of misfortune. They cried out for Jesus in their hours of need, yet I couldn't help but notice that any all of their "miraculous" solutions were the result of human intervention.

Believers prayed for miracles, but they paid for doctors. They asked God for protection, yet they locked their doors and loaded their handguns. They prayed for an "A" on a critical college exam, and then they sweated for days over the study materials. They gave thanks to God for food grown, harvested, and prepared by human hands. They attended the funerals of loved ones killed by disease, malice or misfortune, and they desperately clung to the promise of Romans 8:28, "And we know that God causes all things to work together for good to those who love God, to those who are called according to His purpose."

Tragedy and scandal marked the headlines inside the CCM world every few years, and the faithful would scramble to make sense of it all. I remember the 1982 Los Angeles plane crash of Christian songwriter and evangelist Keith Green. He and two of his children were killed and a nation mourned. Ironically, the brand name for his organization was "Last Days Ministries."

In 1985, Scott Douglas, lead vocalist for the Christian band WhiteHeart was charged with aggravated sexual battery and arrested for statutory rape, ultimately doing prison time and forced to register as a sex offender. The band immediately fired Douglas and spent the next year doing damage control.

Christian rap artist Danny "D-Boy" Rodriguez was shot to death in 1990 while leaving his Dallas apartment. No motive for the murder was ever established.

CCM had a hugely popular Christian comedian, Mike Warnke, who claimed a sordid past as a hard-core drug user and Satanist priest in his autobiography "The Satan Seller." Proclaiming his salvation story worldwide and displaying genuine comedic talent, Warnke sold millions of albums and played to packed convention centers, parlaying his gritty tales of hypodermic needles, blood rituals and (Vietnam) war stories into a multi-million dollar ministry before being exposed as a complete fraud in a 1991 Cornerstone Magazine article.

In '94, Christian superstar Michael English admitted to an affair with Marabeth Jordan (vocalist in another CCM group, "First Call") and spent years in a penitent climb back into the good graces of the religious marketplace. English's career eventually recovered, but First Call disappeared from the radar almost completely. (I personally conducted a KXOJ phone interview with Michael English a couple of years after the scandal, and we slogged through the obligatory questions about his tainted past as he worked to regain a foothold of credibility in the industry.)

A year later, in 1995, Christian icon (and "queen of clean") Sandi Patty admitted an adulterous relationship, and the whole cycle of reclusion, repentance, and re-emergence started all over again.

Christian music's fresh-faced poster child, Amy Grant, announced in 1999 that she was divorcing 17-year husband, Gary Chapman. Many of us in the industry had heard rumors of a connection with Vince Gill (to be fair, a quite-possibly platonic connection), so her marriage to Gill the following year came as little surprise.

And controversial headlines would continue into the new millennium. A fast-rising CCM pop group, Raze, would never recover after vocalist Ja'Marc Davis was convicted of statutory rape of a 14-year-old backup dancer. Popular vocalist Clay Crosse would reveal an addiction to pornography in his 2005 autobiography. Beloved Christian artists Jennifer Knapp and Ray Boltz came out as homosexuals, sending faithful fans into frothy debate over the legitimacy of gays in ministry. (The church is rarely more ham-handed than when tackling the issue of sex.)

Please know that, even now, I take no pride or pleasure in recounting any of these controversies. It was painful to watch my profession and the lives of those involved rocked to the core. With each revelation, each headline, with each shock to the system, the labels, artists and fans did their best to bring sense out of the senselessness.

In almost every case, they were quick to forgive. Their hearts ached with the broken families and shattered reputations. And they struggled to filter the difficult subjects of death, temptation, sexuality, deception, judgment, and punishment through scripture verses and Sunday school lessons.

Tragedy was a reality to the believer, but somehow it was either humankind's fault, an attack of Satan, or somehow part of God's divine plan.

The first time I really began to see this victim mentality objectively was in September, 1997. Yet another horrific headline shocked the American Christian culture. CCM lost another famous face to tragedy, and I started the long, slow journey toward becoming an ex-Christian.

The artist's name was Rich Mullins.

"In the end, religion often attempts to maintain relevance through its final vestiges: hope and comfort."

-    **Wes / Dallas, Texas**

CHAPTER 7
Awesome God

I realize how tempting it is to deify someone posthumously. An icon passes, and the departed becomes bigger than life, adorned in the airbrushed memory banks of those left behind.

But after his 1988 radio hit, "Awesome God," there could be no denying the popularity of CCM artist Rich Mullins. Rich had a few other hits, not as successful, almost all defined by his (extremely) loose singing voice and deft dulcimer riffs. A blockbuster artist he was not, nor did he seem eager to translate "Awesome God" into an opportunity for top billing in his own industry. Rich's folksy, unpolished, demeanor might have been a middle finger to the spit-and-polish marketing machine, or it might have just been a lack of ambition. Whatever it was, millions of Christian music fans responded, anyway. His audience adored him.

I met Rich Mullins in the spring of 1997. He did an in-studio interview on the morning of a KXOJ-sponsored concert. Calm and affable, Rich was so low-key; I couldn't tell if he was sleepy, disinterested, or just shy. His quiet way was pleasant enough, though, and Rich's evening concert was a packed house of appreciative fans who sang every lyric by heart. Our listeners seemed to respond to the unglamorous, organic everyman in Rich Mullins' on-stage persona, and despite some technical glitches, I remember lots of smiles as the lights came up.

A few months later, Rich Mullins was dead.

I was emcee for an outdoor event in a Tulsa suburb when I heard the first whisperings among the attendees about "an accident." Those who've witnessed the chilling metamorphosis of rumor into fact know how these things start. *Someone heard about a car accident. Rich Mullins was involved. No details. Anyone else hear anything? Is he dead or alive? Can we call someone? What happened? It can't be true. It can't be true.*

But on this occasion, it was true. And on the evening of September 19th, 1997, my co-host and I made a late evening drive to the KXOJ main control room to announce to a broadcast audience of thousands that Rich Mullins had been killed. The details we kept mostly to ourselves. They were just too gruesome.

Earlier that night, Rich and songwriting partner Mitch McVicker were unsecured in a jeep traveling on I-39 just north of Bloomington, Illinois when they lost control and flipped the vehicle. Both men were ejected. Rich was thrown onto the highway, too injured to move. An oncoming semi-trailer truck didn't see Rich lying in the road until it was too late. Mullins was struck and killed instantly. Violently. Horribly.

Those outside the culture may not be able to fully understand the grief that overwhelmed the Christian community that day. Rich Mullins was CCM's John Lennon, and I remember watching Jim Marbles, my co-host, KXOJ's comedian and humor mill, unable to speak through his own tears of heartbreak as we broke the news. His reaction, more than anything else, put a lump in my throat, and I struggled to find words of comfort. For him. For the audience. I had no idea what to say.

Because I was charged with updating the KXOJ website, I grabbed a Rich Mullins publicity photo and wrote a short eulogy. I don't remember the text of those paragraphs. Undoubtedly it included the general circumstances of the accident, followed by some poetic words of assurance that Mullins was now being welcomed into the arms of Jesus. I'm sure it contained many of the platitudes heard at Christian funerals, designed to comfort the grieving and inject hope into the despair. No, I don't remember the specific words, but I do remember that, as I typed the headline over Rich's face, I did not feel grief. I felt discomfort. I felt guilt. I felt like a liar.

The headline read, "Welcome Home, Rich."

It was a message designed to comfort. The title implied that, yes, Jesus had called Rich away from this temporary, cruel world to a place where there was no heartache, no confusion, no grief, no pain. Only joy. Bliss. Perfection. Christian music's beloved son had been summoned to a heavenly mansion to receive his crown, to walk streets of gold and to lend his voice to the chorus of angels.

Welcome home, Rich.

The next morning, KXOJ did a Rich Mullins tribute, playing his music and airing phone calls from grieving fans. I remember several listeners thanking us for the online eulogy. Other radio stations around the country had linked the article. Web traffic spiked. Thousands across the nation were responding to the feel-good reassurance that Rich was in a better place, and that somehow our "light and momentary troubles are achieving for us an eternal glory that far outweighs them all. (2 Corinthians 4:17)"

Light and momentary troubles? Excuse me?

That annoying ringing of doubt became a clanging fire alarm in my skull. The more our radio family sang songs of tribute and thanked our heavenly Father for his goodness and mercy, the more I shook my head and stepped away from the increasing insanity of it all. I just couldn't reconcile faith and fact. Matthew 10:29 promised, "Are not two sparrows sold for a penny? Yet not one of them will fall to the ground apart from the will of your Father." So...this was God's will? God was behind it? God had his finger on the button? God had blessed and cultivated his earthly representative, propelled him to the forefront of the entire CCM community, imprinted his life and work onto the hearts of the masses, and then yanked him from this earth in a gruesome accident that would shatter the lives of family and fans across the planet?

And if God wasn't involved, WHY wasn't he involved? Was Rich not worth more than the sparrows of Matthew 10? Was Rich not worth saving? Didn't God's power trump Satan's wiles? Was all of this pain and confusion necessary? What was going on here?

The more I simmered on the idea that God's ingenious master plan would involve twisted steel, the shredded corpse of a mother's son and a closed casket, the more I felt an indignation about the whole charade. Yet I wrestled with the long-engrained mandate that humans aren't supposed to challenge the ways of God. We're all chess pieces in his game, and he can move us as he wishes. It is not for us to question the words of Job 1:21 – "...the LORD gave, and the LORD hath taken away; blessed be the name of the LORD."

Really? We were all pawns to be moved, objects to be rearranged or replaced, insects to be squashed? I found myself wincing at the irrationality and cruelty of such a notion. *Carpe diem, folks, because God could pull the plug at any second. Ripping you from your spouse. From your children. From your parents. From your friends. From your hard-won education and career. From your aspirations and dreams. From everything you hold dear. But the Lord is good. The Lord loves you. Blessed be the name of the Lord.*

I would soon begin directing the same suspicious eye toward other such instances hailed or excused by the faithful, growing increasingly dissatisfied with the immediate acceptance of tragedy and insanity as a loving deity's "mysterious ways."

It has been many years since those dark September days, but Rich Mullins tribute songs, albums, and websites still pepper the CCM landscape. In memory, he remains as beloved as ever, and the Christian community no doubt speaks fondly about the day they will pass through Heaven's pearly gates to join Rich at the savior's side. This lazy, feel-good fantasy ignores the elephant in the room. Is Rich Mullins' "awesome God" a sadist? Incompetent? Or something else?

Years later, I would come to the conclusion that God was indeed "something else."

"It seemed like to be Christian was to deny everything that made me a part of this natural world."

-     Ashley / Atlanta, Georgia

CHAPTER 8
The Towers Fall

In 1999, KXOJ fired me.

After a decade behind the microphone, I'd picked the wrong fight at the wrong time with the wrong person. Years of subtle (and not so subtle) tensions with management finally erupted into red faces and raised voices. They sent me packing with a month's pay and a box filled with my personal effects. I left humiliated.

And I probably deserved it.

Barely in my 30s, I was a young, cocky, insulated and (supposedly) invincible cornerstone of KXOJ's announcer line-up. My personality had always been opinionated, acerbic, and confrontational, and as I became more and more embedded in the tenure machine, those traits amplified. I wasn't a total jerk, but I did have a tendency to be caustic and impatient with those not on my page.

I also struggled with burnout and cynicism, weary of the repetition and the zero-sum ratings game. I was disillusioned with my own industry, so often finding the green rooms populated with flawed, troubled, and sometimes egotistical celebrities far removed from the airbrushed superstars projected to the public. Christian artists were just people, some good, some not, some generous, some selfish, some wonderful, some awful, all propped up by marketing departments and image consultants to win fans, generate album sales, sell concert tickets, and boost revenue.

When the interview microphone was off, many artists admitted their own disillusionment, their "ministries" soured by all of the publicity stunts, the road trips, the grind, the sheer commerce of it all. Christian music was just another sales niche.

I was weary of the game and cynical about the players. I felt like a fraud.

Then I lost a plum job with a steady income, and the fraud became a failure.

I hobbled along for nine months as a freelance producer before getting a second chance as morning host for Clear Channel's LIVE 101.5FM, a Christian Hit Radio format designed to dig into KXOJ's significant market share. (It didn't.)

My host chair sat in the middle of Studio Row, surrounded by all of the other Clear Channel formats: classic rock, Spanish, oldies, pop hits, and sports/talk. Gone was the safe, conservative, squeaky-clean ambience of a family-owned media company. Instead, Mr. Clean found himself dodging second-hand smoke, hard liquor, and f-bombs in a corporate playground unlike anything I'd ever seen.

Most of these hard-drinking, hard-living veterans of "real" radio treated me like fine china. They acted raucously with each other but approached me delicately, self-conscious in their attempts not to offend. They'd walk the hallways and yell obscenities over some incidental thing, then go to the trouble to step backward through my studio door to apologize. I was a member of the Clear Channel clan, but I was too fragile, too meek, too "Christian" to be included in the dirty jokes and late night keggers. I was the religious guy. The conservative guy. The straight arrow. I once heard KMOD's morning host (and Tulsa radio legend) Phil Stone refer to me as a "Quaker." If I had been invited to any wild escapades, no doubt I'd have been the designated driver.

Phil and the crew had no idea that my religious convictions had been muted by years of dissatisfaction. The passion of youth had given way to passive, go-through-the-motions repetition. I'd become accustomed to doubt (my inescapable companion), and I barely bothered to ignore its whispers anymore. I occasionally talked the talk of righteousness, but my own lifestyle betrayed a lack of conviction, a diminished confidence in everything my parents, teachers, and bible lessons had taught me.

I didn't attend church unless invited on a special occasion. I rarely cracked a Bible. I didn't pray before meals or bedtime. I just didn't see the sense of it. Those practices had produced no tangible benefits in youth and early adulthood. Any "blessings" I had could be otherwise explained by hard work, quick thinking, or dumb luck. And it didn't take a rocket scientist to see the cause-and-effect natural laws of the real world consistently trumping the explanations and predictions of zealous pastors and their wide-eyed sheep.

I rationalized my passive stance. I still believed in God, but most church practices and teachings had started to feel pretty silly, so I took a Big Picture approach, ignored the religious routines, and wore God like a Hollywood actor might wear an awareness ribbon; it accomplished nothing, but the display made me feel good. If someone asked if I believed in God, I said "yes." If they inquired where I attended services, I claimed the last church I visited. If they asked me to pray before a meal, I'd weave a beautiful fabric of lofty language (after all, I was a professional communicator) and finish with a hearty "Amen." And few were the wiser.

As morning host of LIVE 101.5, I didn't have to be a preacher or evangelist. I played clean songs that made people feel good, I mingled with enthusiastic listeners, and I put food on the table. No posturing or conviction required. No hard examinations of my embedded beliefs. No altar calls or mission fields. Just radio. Catchy tunes, newscasts, gimmicks and giveaways. In this environment, my skeptical brain and conscience could sleep on the job.

Until September 11th, 2001.

Time has the ability to numb once-sensitive nerves, and the decade after the terrorist attack of 9/11 has (somewhat) muted the shock, the horror, the outrage, and the confusion surrounding that event. Many who dramatically invoke those dark days risk caricature, and for that reason, I hesitated to even include the 9/11 story in my own.

But possibly the single biggest, most impactful, most galvanizing moment in my own crisis of faith came as I sat in my LIVE 101.5FM host chair on studio row. I was three hours into another routine morning show that day, my lazy attitude toward Christianity in full effect when the first news flashes came in.

The initial reports of a WTC plane impact were met with mild surprise, nothing more. We were in radio, the business of bizarre headlines. Every day in the news, some unfortunate (or crazed) person crashed a car, motorcycle, plane, boat, or whatever into a house, storefront, or golf course, and the media barely blinked. When the traffic guy, Jeff, gave me the news, I figured a student pilot had blown a single-engine Cessna through some office windows and earned himself a Darwin Award. I certainly didn't feel any sense of alarm.

Within moments, of course, that would change.

By the time the second plane struck the South Tower, Clear Channel Tulsa's 9th floor offices boiled with intensity. All six radio stations were on high alert, interrupting all standard programming to give minute-by-minute updates on the chaos of lower Manhattan. Our general manager ultimately ordered all station signals linked together to broadcast a single feed, one stream of information split six ways.

Voices shouted down hallways. Producers scoured the internet. There were mad searches for offices with televisions. It wasn't quite panic. It was a scramble for some hard data buried within the avalanche of blind, desperate speculation.

Of course, we would soon see beyond the images of billowing smoke and wreckage and into the sinister forces behind the carnage. The cocoon of security that Americans took for granted had been shredded by nineteen terrorists with box cutters, and the sheltered children of the free world stood frozen like stunned animals in the path of a train. The towers fell, and we were helpless. The Pentagon burned, and we were helpless. Flight 93 plummeted to the ground, and we were helpless.

Helpless. Powerless. And afraid. Of course, this is when we pray.

At the height of the crisis, just after the North Tower collapsed into rubble, several ladies from the business office walked into my studio. They'd come from another part of the Clear Channel facility directly to my door. They needed comfort. They sought protection. To these four teary-eyed, trembling women, I was no longer the fine china, the sheltered church kid, the Quaker. I was a hotline to God. I was the first person they thought of when everything hit the fan. And they had a request. "Please pray for us."

Still stunned from the insanity of what I was seeing on every TV channel, I looked over at them blankly and sheepishly agreed. We all formed a circle and joined hands, and while I can't remember the exact wording in my prayer, I have no doubt it echoed thousands of other desperate pleas that day. I wrapped my radio voice around phrases I'd said and heard so often in times of crisis, and I'm sure it sounded something like this:

"Dear Lord, we ask that you protect us in this horrible time. We pray that you'll be with those in distress. Please help the wounded see their way to safety. Please help the rescue workers find and save those who are trapped. Please comfort the families of those who have been killed. Please be with our country and protect us against any future attacks. We ask that you'll put your hand of protection around us. Deliver us from evil. Give us guidance and direction. Help us get through this tragedy, and bring those responsible to justice. We know you have a plan, and we believe that you'll bring something good out of this situation. Just be with us. Help us. Give us peace. Comfort us. Direct us. We ask these things in the name of Jesus, amen."

It was performance more than prayer. A cliché. An empty cry to an empty sky. And as we all exchanged hugs and the women filtered out into the hallway, I just sat there, quiet, alone, overwhelmed by a single, inescapable thought: "We are kidding ourselves."

We were all still tumbling in the avalanche of anger and tears that morning, but even as I'd prayed aloud, I felt it was ridiculous to beg for divine protection as thousands lay dead amid the twisted steel and burning jet fuel. Any benevolent, omniscient, omnipotent deity could have easily prevented the fires of terror from ever being lit. Did it not occur to God to invalidate some passports? To afflict the Al Qaeda operatives with palsy? To cause airline maintenance issues on the flights involved and prevent takeoff? Hell, God could've locked all nineteen terrorists in a monster traffic jam and busted the whole operation.

Yet God was a non-participant. Invisible. Nowhere to be found. And this was where Christian evangelists Jerry Falwell, Pat Robertson, and their ilk gave their own astounding (and wildly offensive) explanation. God did not participate or prevent the horror of September 11th because…(wait for it)…America had allowed the proliferation of abortion clinics and homosexuals.

Falwell appeared on the Christian Broadcasting Network's "700 Club" (hosted by Pat Robertson himself) to proclaim, "God continues to lift the curtain and allow the enemies of America to give us probably what we deserve."[5] He and Robertson blasted the ACLU, abortion supporters, gays, lesbians and all who had attempted to "secularize America" as the reason the hand of protection was removed from us. We deserved it. We had it coming. One Nation Under God was now being spanked like a disobedient child. We had ignored the warnings about evil deeds and evildoers, so God turned his back on us as we burned in the fires of our own rebellious iniquity.

Robertson and Falwell muted these assertions in the months ahead,

---

5   By John F. Harris Washington Post Staff Writer Friday, September 14, 2001; Page C03

but their message was clear. The terrorist attack wouldn't have happened if America's citizens had adhered to scriptural teachings and honored the God we printed on our dollar bills and invoked in our pledge of allegiance. Hell hath no fury like a jealous deity scorned.

This was the mentality of many Christians in my own circle. We were the problem. We screwed up the world. We blew it.

Another popular assertion was that God was using more of this "light and momentary affliction" to turn us from our rebellion and bring the prodigal sons and daughters home. It never occurred to the faithful that God's intent (or existence) was eligible for challenge.

So while God tormented the planet like a spoiled child might torment the neighbor's cat, Christians gave thanks that it wasn't much worse, self-blaming in the language of a battered spouse. *He only punishes me because he loves me. He wouldn't do it if I didn't deserve it. Sometimes the best love is tough love. He knows what's best for me. I just can't leave him.*

A famous atheist t-shirt says, "Science flies you to the moon. Religion flies you into buildings." But as the dust settled on those events, I wasn't yet focused on the dangerous religious fanaticism that plunged airliners into the World Trade Center. I hadn't seen religion as a proactive, destructive force (I even defended "peace-loving" Muslims in a late-September radio interview).

Rather, I saw 9/11 as a decidedly human experience. Humans planned the attack. Humans died in it. Humans responded, climbing the stairwells of the burning towers in heroic attempts of rescue. Humans hijacked United flight 93, and humans prevented it from reaching its intended target. Humans treated the wounded. Humans comforted the grieving. Humans mourned and buried their dead. Everything could be explained, not with God, but by observing action and reaction in a world devoid of any detectable supernatural agency.

God's name had certainly been invoked, for evil by the architects of the attack, and for good by those who discovered random silver linings in this jet-black cloud. God was certainly on the tip of everyone's tongue. The terrorists martyred themselves to be rewarded by God. The meek prayed for protection from God. The pulpit preachers ranted about judgment from God.

And I kept wondering why the guest of honor never showed up. He created our world and its inhabitants. He put the wheels in motion. He came to earth that we might have life, and have it abundantly (John 10:10). Yet death prevailed, and humans were the only palpable forces for both good and evil. God wasn't the architect. God wasn't the hero. God wasn't the villain. God turned out to be "something else." A giant flashing zero.

Where was he? We were his children. Wasn't this his party?

"I'd tell myself 'I don't think there is a god, but I won't say it, just in case he is real…and listening.'"

- **Theresa / Maryland**

CHAPTER 9
Dormant in the Faith

I'm reminded of a video interview I conducted in February, 2011 with an ex-Mormon whose doubts about his religion caused him to go "dormant in the faith" several years before his ultimate apostasy.

Dormant in the faith. Exactly. This is what often happens to believers when they can no longer stomach the platitudes, the promises, the requirements, the contradictions, the corruption and the sheer theater of their doctrine and traditions. They don't immediately become emboldened by the lightning strike of epiphany and turn on a dime. They're not ready to remove God from the equation and brandish the atheist "A" symbol on their sleeve. It's too unthinkable. Too big a step. Too far to fall.

So instead, they just filter themselves out of the equation. They're like the university student that never attends class but still has his name on the rolls. Still part of the club, just not active.

This is what happened to me.

9/11 had certainly snapped me out of my coma, but becoming fully lucid would take years. Instead of getting serious about addressing my questions and concerns, I simply checked out. Avoidance was certainly easier than stirring things up. God became like the relative that never attended the family reunions. We were supposed to be connected, but since God never showed up, he was never really missed, and as this disconnect became more evident, I was glad for the opportunity to jump out of the religious broadcasting chair.

Christian Hit Radio LIVE 101.5FM failed after only eighteen months but Clear Channel gave me another morning slot at 92.1 KISS-FM before I finally said goodbye to full-time radio altogether in 2004. loved broadcasting, but radio was a shrinking business, and I wanted to make my exit before I became an unemployment statistic.

For years, I'd watched many veteran radio announcers being given their pink slips. Legendary local voices were being replaced by (much cheaper) syndicated shows and computer automation. Local broadcasters had given decades to their professions and city, only to be replaced by a computer and some inexpensive, out-of-state free lancer with a home studio.

I'll tell you a little secret. Flip through your FM radio dial, and there's a high probability that your "local" disc jockey not only lives in another state, but he almost certainly pre-recorded the entire show the day (or several days) before. If you hear your announcer give the time, the weather, or details about local events, it's because the information is available to him on a computer screen. He's blindly reading information from hundreds or thousands of miles away, often pre-recording radio shows in bare feet and pajamas in a tucked away corner of his house, and nobody is the wiser.

Nobody's wiser except, of course, for the broadcast companies that save copious amounts of money by leaving the local studios dark and piping in canned radio shows on the cheap. And from a business perspective, I really can't blame them. Why pay a full-time salary (plus benefits) to an egotistical, veteran, local announcer when you can contract some young, hungry freelancer for $600 a month?

Decades ago, broadcast music options for the consumer were few. But as internet stations and satellite radio began their post-millennium surge, the world was shrinking. Sirius and XM were becoming available on car stereos. Listeners could populate their own commercial-free playlists via iTunes and Spotify. Big-name broadcast meteorologists were bleeding listeners and viewers to WeatherBug. News headlines were a single click from any computer.

Radio companies everywhere tightened their belts as audience shares slipped away. And the local radio disc jockey watched helplessly as he became expendable, a line-item on the budget sheet, a warm body filling a temporary chair.

In 2003, I saw the writing on the wall when a co-worker got the axe and ended up sacking groceries part-time to pay the bills. After three decades as a radio icon, he'd become the guy double-bagging your milk and frozen chicken. The business had changed, minimizing personnel and maximizing technology, and it was only a matter of time until any one of us might be called back to the manager's office for a pink slip and a severance check. So I became proactive about my future, saying goodbye to radio production at Clear Channel and jumping into video production for a local media company. After fourteen years as a full-time radio broadcaster, I walked away.

I'd continue dipping my toe into the radio pool as a voice-track disc jockey, one of "those guys" with a home studio and a low price point. I figured I could either helplessly watch from the sidelines, or I could adapt to this new business model and create my own opportunities.

The irony? The freelance radio jobs that came my way were for Christian broadcasting companies. The icing on the cake? My new video production job served a huge church clientele. So while I had slowly started to outgrow the ill-fitting skin of religious belief, I had just signed on to serve the very church culture I found so frustrating. This arrangement was a marriage of convenience. I was able to implement my *gifts* to *bless* these *ministries* without ever having to endure long-term commitment in a local church, and I'd be using my talents (ala Matthew 25) in a way pleasing to God. I was doing God's good work, but I got to phone it in.

I had surfed that wave of hypocrisy for years…until I finally decided I couldn't take it anymore.

"Learning changed my life and gave me the resources and evidence to piece together all the reasons why I am an atheist."

- **Marisa / Indiana**

CHAPTER 10
The Hitch Slap

In 2004, I knew very little about author and journalist Christopher Hitchens. I'd seen him as a regular guest on Dennis Miller's CNBC talk show, and he was certainly erudite and impressive. I enjoyed the thick, witty verbal exchanges and easy chemistry he and Miller had on-camera. Hitchens conducted himself with a remarkably cool and cocky authority, evidently the smartest guy in the room. But the panel topics were mostly the bland political fodder of the day, and I'd written the man off as another media pundit in a network news culture suffocating with them.

Fast-forward a few years. Christopher Hitchens' book "The Portable Atheist" was pushing the buttons and raising the hackles of apologists worldwide, piquing my curiosity. And while I'd been softly tip-toeing around my "God issues," Hitchens gleefully brandished a giant middle finger toward all things religious. He reveled in the shit-storm. The guy was fearless, well-spoken, with an encyclopedic knowledge of things religious, historical, and political.

A YouTube search led me to the video of a debate between Christopher Hitchens and Rabbi Shmuley Boteach. The exchange took place at New York's 92nd Street Y on January 30th, 2008. I certainly wasn't Jewish, nor was I a defender of Jewish teachings or traditions, but Rabbi Boteach was a famous syndicated columnist, author of over 20 books, a prolific speaker, a frequent TV personality, and Newsweek had recently dubbed him "the most famous rabbi in America." Certainly, this religious *expert* had the chops to defend the God of the Bible. I'd never seen a debate like this, and I thought to myself, "This oughta be good."

It *was* good. But not in the way I had anticipated.

I found Boteach embarrassing. Despite his passion, his lofty proclamations and passages from the Torah and an undeniable charisma and ease with language, Boteach's only real weapon in this tet-a-tet was enthusiasm. Emotion. Verve. And instead of demonstrating solid proofs to support the existence of God, the rabbi was instead focused on highlighting controversial passages in his antagonist's book, peppering his prepared remarks with ad hominems like, "Christopher Hitchens is a secular fundamentalist fanatic."

When Rabbi Boteach did offer up a defense of the Almighty, the talking points were variations of hackneyed, clichéd assertions I've since heard a thousand times: *Life without a higher power is meaningless and void. Morality doesn't exist inside the evolutionary model. The human eye is too complex to have evolved. Scientist X believes in an intelligent designer.*

Then, a mere thirty minutes into the debate, Boteach attempted to discredit evolution by comparing the philosophies and writings of Charles Darwin to those of Adolf Hitler.

Adolf Hitler?

At that moment, you could've fit my knowledge of Darwin in a matchbox, but throughout my adult life, I'd always felt that an invocation of Hitler was (in American football lingo) the Hail Mary pass of a losing team. I'd watched speeches where some Pez-headed politician, celebrity activist, or zealous preacher would toss the Hitler grenade from the podium, and it always rang false. Branding the opposition with the name of last century's (arguably) most infamous tyrant was merely a provocation, a hot-button, the desperate flailing of drowning credibility.

In the following years, I would soon come to learn that Adolf Hitler did not endorse or champion evolution but instead practiced eugenics (a far different concept). Raised Roman Catholic and ultimately embracing Christianity, Hitler would invoke God throughout his life and in his writings: "Hence today I believe that I am acting in accordance with the will of the Almighty Creator: by defending myself against the Jew, I am fighting for the work of the Lord." –Adolf Hitler (Mein Kampf) [6]

Boteach's linking of Darwin and Hitler was factually vacant and disingenuous.

As I watched the debate play on, the question lingered. Was the religious movement so desperate that it would place Charles Darwin - a naturalist - in the same category with history's most horrific monsters? As I would soon learn, the answer was, "Absolutely."

How did Christopher Hitchens handle these inflammatory charges from the good rabbi? Deftly. Defiantly. Easily. His measured remarks and rebuttals stood in quiet contrast to the grand inflections and amplitude of his opponent, adding a gravitas to challenges against the validity and morality of scripture that had never before appeared on my radar: *There's scientific evidence of the Big Bang, observable*

---

6   Adolf Hitler, Mein Kampf, Ralph Mannheim, ed., New York: Mariner Books, 1999, p. 65.

in a phenomenon known as The Hubble Constant? Human DNA reveals commonalities with all living things, including vegetation, pointing to common ancestry? There are computer models that reveal how the human eye evolved? The Bible is demonstrably false and filled with "horrors?" What horrors?

I was on the edge of my seat. I'd never before seen God challenged so directly. I'd certainly had my share of issues with the attributes and involvement of God, but to assert that he was merely a phantom birthed from the primitive imaginations of superstitious men? Unthinkable!

You may laugh at my naiveté, but the deep roots of indoctrination had kept me, like so many others, from straying too far from established boundaries. Christian children were taught to never directly challenge, tempt, or "test the Lord thy God" Since our earliest memories, we were told to love God but also fear him. God would save us but could also punish us. God was a merciful God. God was a jealous God. God knew everything. God saw everything. And God would not be mocked.

But that day, I observed mockery in full, living, glorious color. Christopher Hitchens had directly and gleefully reduced Christ to caricature, and when the audience gave the final ovation for these two men, I couldn't escape the feeling that God's ambassador had just gotten handily spanked by a columnist at Vanity Fair.

I immediately scoured YouTube for as much Hitchens as I could find. Debates. Speeches. Interviews. I couldn't get enough. And the Hitchens clips led me to discover other high-profile soldiers in this crusade against religion, names I'd never heard before: Richard Dawkins. Sam Harris. Daniel Dennett. Dan Barker.

Who were these men? Why had I never heard of them? Had they been hidden under wraps, sheltered from mainstream audiences, insulated from the rest of the world?

As I would soon come to realize, they weren't the ones who had been living in a bubble. I'd spent almost four decades taking up oxygen on this planet, and not once had I been properly introduced to the perspectives of legitimate scientists, philosophers, and thinkers. My worldview had never, not once, been challenged in any meaningful way. Throughout my life, God had always been the beginning of the discussion, and all facts, figures, statistics, and scientific discoveries were viewed through rose-colored God Glasses. Every evidential piece that didn't fit the God puzzle was either altered to conform or discarded.

Finally, I'd heard perspectives that sounded sensible, albeit uncomfortable to entertain. But these people were atheists!

The Christians in my life rarely spoke about non-believers except in the broad context of our Great Commission (Matthew 28) to preach the gospel to every nation. Christians sought out and ministered to The Lost. Of course, the word "lost" implies that the non-believer can be found, rescued, delivered, saved. The undercurrent of this thinking is that these unfortunate, wandering souls are simply waiting for Christianity to arrive and present God's good news, thankful for the chance to slough off the bondage of sin and experience the bliss of salvation.

To the average Christian, The Lost are usually people of other faiths, cultures, or traditions, or perhaps they've attended church without ever saying the salvation prayer. The Lost are hell-bound, but they are still salvageable. The Lost can be found.

The term "atheist" carries a more sinister tone, conjuring up visions of moral anarchy and outright evil. I hardly ever heard "atheist" used in everyday conversation, and on the rare occasions any of my Christian friends or family members uttered the word, it hissed out of their mouths with disdain. Attttheissssst.

In the mind of the faithful (at least here in the American Bible Belt), the atheist is the poster child for darkness and chaos, a rebellious, rudderless, angry, sad, pathetic malcontent who is ill-equipped to understand the God-originated concepts of joy, love, goodness, truth, family, life, and death. The atheist is the poison in the well. The atheist is the molester of minds that children should be shielded from. The atheist lurks in the shadows of upright society, a counter-culture anomaly, a freak.

But these atheists didn't fit the stereotype at all. In video after video, Hitchens, Dawkins, Dennett, Harris and Barker came off as informed, thoughtful, humorous and enthusiastic. I quietly admired the unabashed defiance these men displayed. Completely unconcerned about lightning bolts from an angry sky, they shined the spotlight up toward the heavens and snickered, "Bring it!"

I had to go deeper. I had to know more. Within days, I purchased an intriguing book from Amazon.com and began devouring its pages. The book was written by a former evangelist named Charles Templeton, and it would change my life.

A personal friend of Billy Graham, Charles Templeton was a popular Canadian minister who had apparently found himself in conflict with the very bible teachings he had once espoused, ultimately rejecting them and announcing – very publicly – that he was an atheist. His story sounded fascinating, so I picked up "Farewell to God:

My Reasons for Rejecting the Christian Faith."

I devoured it.

It was the first written critique of scripture that I'd ever encountered Up to that time, any God-related books in my zip code came from authors like James Dobson, Chuck Swindoll, Max Lucado, Rick Warren, and Josh McDowell. Those books had been deferential sugary love letters from God's fan club and stood in stark contrast to Templeton's critical approach.

"Farewell to God" challenged the facts, physics, historical accuracy and credibility of Noah's Ark, the six-day Creation, Moses' exodus from Egypt, Jesus' birth, the crucifixion account, etc. The cherished Bible stories of my childhood were dismantled one by one, not with anger and malice, but thoughtfully and carefully. The dominoes were starting to fall.

Templeton exposed stories in the Old Testament I never knew existed, revealing an impulsive, petty, bloodthirsty God never alluded to in the sheltered halls of Sunday church. Verse by verse, chapter by chapter, story by story, I saw rape, incest, slavery, and death not as wicked acts committed by sinful humans, but as the edicts and actions of a monstrous God who reveled in the mass graves of the disobedient.

When I finished the book, I just sat there, embarrassed. As far back as I could remember, bibles had cluttered my bookshelves, had been given and received as gifts, had been quoted from and sworn upon, yet I had never taken a long, thorough, objective look at the pages within. For almost every Christian I knew (including myself), the Bible was a decorative item, something to put on the nightstand, a centerpiece to be displayed, a prop to be carried under the arm. It was the song we sang as children: *"The B-I-B-L-E. Now that's the book for me. I stand up on the word of God. The B-I-B-L-E."*

My next book was Dan Barker's "Godless," another raw, autobiographical account of a prominent evangelist who could no longer stomach God and his scriptures. Again, I absorbed the pages in long sessions as the hours ticked by.

From "Godless," I tore through Richard Dawkins' "The God Delusion," Daniel Dennett's "Breaking the Spell," and Sam Harris' "Letter to a Christian Nation" in rapid succession. These books offered up a litany of facts, informed opinions, and scripture verses I'd never encountered before, and the groggy lethargy of my religious belief was quickly giving way to lucidity, clarity, epiphany. After decades of sleep, I was waking up.

My friends expressed concern that I had become "obsessed." I can understand why. I *was* obsessed. And as loved ones looked on with increasing panic, I filled every free moment with atheist books, websites, and videos. I was compensating for thirty years of holding my breath. I was the dehydrated man drinking deep. I was energized and driven.

With this heightened awareness and newly-formed (evolved?) critical eye, I decided to take a long, fresh, objective look at the Holy Bible. And like so many apostates before me, I would discover that the ultimate catalyst for my rejection of God would come from the pages of scripture themselves.

"Teaching hatred to children could be the gravest offense to our species."

-    **Cordelle / Cincinnati, OH**

CHAPTER 11
The Edge of the Sword

The God of the Bible endorses rape. No kidding.

Within the pages of Christian scripture, God, Yahweh, Elohim, El Shaddai, Yeshua, Jehovah-Jireh, the Alpha and Omega condoned and sometimes even instructed the kidnapping and sexual assault of women.

As a child, I'd heard a dozen times the account of Lot (Genesis 19:15-23). A righteous man was saved from the destruction of the wicked city of Sodom, his wife turned into a pillar of salt for disobediently turning around to look. This story was classic Sunday school fodder. Man was wicked. God was merciful. Obedience was rewarded. Disobedience was punished. Justice was done.

Meanwhile, hidden in plain sight a few verses earlier, Lot, God's righteous servant, had offered to protect his angel guests by offering up his own virgin daughters to be raped by a crazed mob. (Genesis 19:6-8) "Lot went outside to meet them and shut the door behind him and said, 'No, my friends. Don't do this wicked thing. Look, I have two daughters who have never slept with a man. Let me bring them out to you, and you can do what you like with them. But don't do anything to these men, for they have come under the protection of my roof.'"

How, exactly, does "Take my daughters. They're virgins!" constitute righteousness? Can you imagine any moral father saying something so obscene? Wouldn't you as a parent throw yourself between your children and harm, even at the cost of your own life? A frothing mob pounds at your door for the purpose of sexual violence, and you fling your daughters into the firing line like skeet?

Then, as Lot was indeed rescued and rewarded after this revolting display, his wife was struck down by God (Genesis 19:26) for the heinous crime of looking over her shoulder.

The story gets even better. Lot's daughters got their father liquored up (Genesis 19:34) so they could take turns having sex with him to "preserve our family line through our father." Well, of course. When you have baby fever and there are no male prospects in the immediate area, it's perfectly acceptable to date rape your own parent. God offered no word of protest over this incestuous rendezvous. Perhaps he was still fuming about those icky homosexuals back in Sodom.

In Numbers 31:17-18, God continued his promotion of sexual violence by instructing Moses to kill all of the male Midianite children and "kill every woman who has slept with a man, but save for yourselves every girl who has never slept with a man." Save the virgins for yourselves? Really? Apologists insist that the soldiers bore no malice nor intended any violence to these teenage girls, also shrugging off the kidnapping angle and lauding God's mercy for sparing lives. I suppose you can talk yourself into believing that the kidnappers blessed their abductees with joyous lives of equality free from strife, but you'd have to be hitting the Mescaline pretty hard.

Deuteronomy 20:13-14 had God laying out the rules for battle, instructing the slaughter of all of the men. Women, children, livestock and possessions could be taken as "plunder for yourselves." The following chapter encouraged the taking of enemy women as wives if a soldier was "attracted to her," complete with Yahweh's direction to "shave her head, trim her nails and put aside the clothes she was wearing when captured" (Deuteronomy 21:12-13). Nice. Kidnap her, alter her appearance, and claim her. Not happy with the woman you abducted after slaughtering her previous husband? Release her like a stray cat.

The list goes on and on. Rape victims actually received a death sentence in Deuteronomy 22:23-24, punishment because they "did not scream for help." The 28th chapter instructed that a rape victim must marry the rapist, with the rapist paying 50 silver pieces to the father as compensation. 2 Samuel 12:11-12 had Yahweh hand-delivering wives to other men to be raped, saying "This is what the LORD says; 'Out of your own household I am going to bring calamity on you. Before your very eyes I will take your wives and give them to one who is close to you, and he will sleep with your wives in broad daylight.'" Zechariah 14 announced that "a day of the LORD is coming, Jerusalem, when your possessions will be plundered and divided up within your very walls. I will gather all the nations to Jerusalem to fight against it; the city will be captured, the houses ransacked, and the women raped."

Throughout scripture, women were burned alive (Leviticus 21), had their limbs hacked off (Deuteronomy 25:11-12), were shunned as unclean (Leviticus 12:5), and were relegated to the shadows of the man's authority (1 Timothy 2:11-14). Those women who weren't branded as whores and harlots were given strict instructions to shut up, remain submissive, and know their place in the pecking order. "For man did not come from woman, but woman from man; neither was man created for woman, but woman for man." (1 Corinthians 11:8-9)

I'm ashamed to admit that these passages were new to me. I'd been baptized in the gooey poetry of Ephesians 5:25, where husbands were instructed to love their wives as Christ loved the church. 1 Corinthians 13 (the love chapter) had been recited at countless weddings and Valentine's Day church functions, punctuating the misty-eyed romance of it all with the climactic 13th verse, "And now these three remain: faith, hope and love. But the greatest of these is love.'

Somehow, my pastors and teachers had neglected to teach about God's evil twin - the sexually-obsessed executioner who regarded women as the mere spoils of war, objects to be plundered, second-class and expendable.

And those passages were the tip of the tip of the iceberg. God's contempt spread well beyond women to anyone who rankled his petty sensibilities. Reading the verses of scripture without a deferential filter, I discovered example after example of a bloodthirsty and murderous dictator:

- Exodus 32:27 - After seeing the golden calf, God commanded the Levites, "Each man strap a sword to his side. Go back and forth through the camp from one end to the other, each killing his brother and friend and neighbor." Three thousand were slaughtered, and God was pleased.

- Numbers 15:32-36 - A man gathered sticks for a fire on the Sabbath. By God's command, he was stoned to death.

- Numbers 16:27-33 – The men were rebellious, so God caused the earth to open and swallow up the men, wives and children.

- Numbers 25:9 - A plague from God killed 24,000.

- Judges 7:19-25 – Under God's direction, Gideon's army

defeated the Midianites. They killed and decapitated their princes and delivered the heads to Gideon.

- Judges 11:29-39 - Jephthah cooked his beloved daughter on an altar as a sacrifice to God for giving him victory in battle.

- 1 Samuel 6:19 – Some of the men of Beth Shemesh looked into the Ark of the Covenant. God killed all seventy of them.

- 1 Samuel 15:7-8 – God commanded Saul to attack the Amalekites and "totally destroy everything that belongs to them. Do not spare them; put to death men and women, children and infants, cattle and sheep, camels and donkeys."

- 2 Samuel 6:6-7 – The oxen carrying the Ark of God stumbled, and Uzzah reached out to steady it. God punished his "irreverent act" by killing him where he stood.

- 1 Kings 13:15-24 – A prophet lied to a man, telling him it was fine to eat bread and drink water in a place the Lord had previously told him not to. The deceived man ate and drank there. God sent a lion to kill him, "and his body was thrown down on the road."

- 2 Chronicles 13:17 – God delivered the Israelites to Abijah and Judah--500,000 enemy dead.

- Ezekiel 20:26 – Israel rebelled, and God's punishment was sobering. "I let them become defiled through their gifts- the sacrifice of every firstborn- that I might fill them with horror so they would know that I am the Lord."

Fill them with *horror*?

There was plenty of horror in the book of Joshua, the book that contained the celebrated Joshua's miraculous victory at Jericho as they blew the trumpets and the walls of the city fell. I still remember the song we sang as children in Sunday school:

Joshua fought the battle of Jericho
Jericho
Jericho
Joshua fought the battle of Jericho
And the walls came tumbling down!

This catchy little ditty conveniently ignored the specifics of what happened AFTER the walls came tumbling down. Under God's direction, Joshua's army became a blood-drunk horde of executioners, putting men, women, teenagers and infants to the "edge of the sword." The soldiers then pillaged the gold, silver, bronze, and iron for God and burned the city. This scene of carnage would be repeated throughout the next several chapters:

- Joshua 7:19-26: Ai conquered. Achan's sons, daughters, cattle, donkeys, sheep and possessions were taken to the Valley of Achor where they were stoned and burned.

- Joshua 8:22-25: 12,000 men and women were slaughtered

- Joshua 10:10-27: all of the Gibeonites killed

- Joshua 10:28: all in Makkedah killed

- Joshua 10:30: all of the city of Libnah was "put to the sword"

- Joshua 10:32-33: all in Lachish killed

- Joshua 10:34-35: all in Eglon killed

- Joshua 10:36-37: killed the king of Hebron, its villages and every citizen. "They left no survivors"

- Joshua 10:38-39: all of Debir killed

- Joshua 11:6: God commanded Joshua to defeat the enemy at the Waters of Merom. "You are to hamstring their horses" (a horrific act of animal cruelty) "and burn their chariots"

Funny. Sunday school teachers never taught us THOSE songs.

The fun continued, as I dove deeper to discover that Christianity's sacred texts showed God endorsing slavery and the beating of slaves. Exodus 21:20-21 actually allowed masters to physically assault their slaves, providing that the beaten slaves were able to stand after a few days. God's law in Exodus 21:7 actually provided instructions for fathers selling their daughters into slavery. And true to form when it came to women, Leviticus 27 decreed that female slaves were worth half the value of male ones.

Some Bible stories were just bizarre. 1 Samuel 18:25-27 explained how David gave King Saul a dowry of 200 Philistine foreskins to earn the hand of Saul's daughter, Michal, in marriage. (I'm sure this spiced things up during the gift opening at the wedding reception. "Penis flesh? Oh, it's lovely!"). Deuteronomy 23:1 instructed that "No one whose testicles are crushed or whose male organ is cut off shall enter the assembly of the Lord." Genesis 38:8-10 had God telling a guy named Onan to have sex with his brother's wife in order to produce a child, and when Onan instead pulled out and ejaculated on the ground, God killed him. Deuteronomy 25:11-12 dictated that, if a man was in a fight with another man and his wife intervened by seizing the opponent by his genitals, the woman's hand was to be hacked off at the wrist.

Foreskins? Testicals? Semen? Genitals? For an omnipotent master of the universe, God sure had a conspicuous (and violent) obsession with the penis.

Stories like these (and so many others) were extremely disturbing, but it was even more disturbing to watch Christians excuse them away, offering up lazy explanations that would be rejected wholesale if applied to the Qur'an or another religion's holy book: *It was a different time. His ways are not our ways. Some of those stories are just metaphors. Just stick to the New Testament. He's God, so he can do whatever he wants.*

Apparently, mere humans cannot possibly comprehend an infinitely superior Being. Biblical curses, decapitation, kidnapping, rape, infanticide, human sacrifice, and rivers of blood were all part of a greater plan that we mortals cannot digest. And, according to the armchair apologists, even if God *had* acted with bigotry, misogyny, petty jealousy, frothing rage, and cruel vengeance, it's his universe, his game, his rules, and the obedient Christian is expected to simply fall in lock-step, shut his mouth, and trust that Father knows best.

As I continued to dig, I found that many of the scriptures that weren't wildly offensive were either contradictory or demonstrably false.

The Nativity Story

- Matthew 1:20 declares that the angel appeared to Joseph. Luke 1:28 says the angel appeared to Mary.

- Luke 2:1-3 says that Quirinius issued a decree for a census, but the book of Matthew mentions no census, and Quirinius' census didn't take place until 6CE in Joseph's local tax district, requiring only the male heads of households to register.

- Matthew 2:13-16 declares that Mary and Joseph fled to Egypt to escape Herod's death edict, yet Luke 2:39 says they returned to Nazareth with no mention of Herod at all.

- The virgin birth story is actually based on a mistranslation of the Hebrew word, "almah," which translates "young woman of marriageable age" and could have been applied to any young woman without the inclusion of an immaculate conception backstory. (The Hebrew word for virgin is actually "bethulah.") Interestingly, several pre-Christ gods were also said to be born of a virgin, including Perseus and Romulus.

- "We Three Kings" (a popular Christmas legend and song) isn't factually tethered to the nativity story. Matthew 2:1-2 calls them magi – or illusionists – and there's no mention of the number three anywhere. Contrast this with Luke 2:25, which says that shepherds, not magi, journeyed to see baby Jesus in the manger

Can Man Be Righteous?

- Genesis 7:1 says that Noah was righteous. Job 2:3 says Job was righteous. Luke 1:6 says Zechariah and Elizabeth were righteous. James 5:16 says "some men" were righteous. 1 John 3:7 says that Christians can become righteous. But Romans 3:10 states clearly, "As it is written, 'There is no one righteous, not even one.'"

Who Is Punished For Sins?

- Ezekiel 18:20 asserts that the penalty of sin lies solely with the sinner. "The son shall not bear the iniquity of the father." But Exodus 20:5 declares that sin contaminates generations. "I the Lord thy God am a jealous God, visiting the iniquity of the fathers upon the children unto the third and fourth generation."

Does God Keep Anger Forever?

- Jeremiah 3:12, "...for I am merciful, saith the Lord, and will not keep anger forever." But in the very same book chapter 17 verse 4 declares, "Ye have kindled a fire in mine anger, which shall burn forever."

Who Brought The Capernaum Centurion's Request to Jesus?

- Matthew 8:5 says it's the centurion himself. Luke 7:3 states that the centurion sent elders. Luke 7:6 (same book and chapter as "elders") says the centurion sent friends.

Where Did Jesus Go After Feeding The 5,000?

- Mark 6:53 says that Jesus and the disciples went to Gennesaret. John 6:24-25 says they went to Capernaum.

Where Did The Anointing of Christ Take Place?

- Matthew 26:6-7 tells us that the anointing happened "in Bethany in the home of a man known as Simon the Leper." Oil is placed on Jesus' head by an unnamed woman. Luke 7:36-37 says that oil was placed on Jesus' feet, not his head, at the house of a Pharisee in Galilee. John 12:3 says it wasn't an unnamed woman who anointed Jesus, but Mary.

Did The Cursed Fig Tree Wither Immediately?

- Matthew 21:19 says the tree withered immediately. Mark 11:20 gives the contradictory account, "And in the morning, as they passed by, they saw the fig tree dried up from the roots." Also, why would Jesus be angry that the fig tree had nothing for him to eat? Wouldn't an omniscient deity know when fig season is? (Bible scholars rationalize that Christ was using the tree as a metaphor for the nation of Israel, but if that's the case, it's uncanny how this god-man so often eschews plain speaking in favor of confusing symbolism.)

What Were Jesus' Last Words On The Cross?

- Matthew 27:46, "My God, my God, why hast thou forsaken me?" This contrasts Luke 23:46, where Jesus' last words are, "Father, into thy hands I commend my spirit" and John 19:30, "It is finished."

Who Were The First Visitors To Jesus' Tomb?

- Matthew 28:1 says it was Mary Magdalene and the other Mary. Mark 16:1 says there was a third person, Salome. Luke 24:10 lists the two Marys, Joanna and "the others." John 20:1 mentions only Mary Magdalene.

How Did Judas Die?

- Matthew 27:3-8 states that Judas hanged himself. Acts 1:16-19 says, "Now this man purchased a field with the reward of iniquity; and falling headlong, he burst asunder in the midst, and all his bowels gushed out."

The above examples are just a few of many, and for the first time in my life, I was examining the different accounts of identical events side by side, astounded and embarrassed that I hadn't noticed the discrepancies before.

I brought these Bible-borne examples of bloodlust and incongruity

to the attention of friends and family, only to be met with shrugs
and indifference. Nobody had satisfactory answers. Nobody joined
my chorus of concern. Nobody really cared. And their lives moved
forward without a hitch. That was it. Happy scriptures were embraced and extolled, and nasty verses were blinked away. If there
were problems with the Bible, Christians didn't know.

And the worst part? They didn't want to know.

"I was told to go talk to the Pastor. I told him there were parts of the bible I didn't understand. After 45 minutes of ducking my questions, the Pastor angrily told me, 'You just have to take it on faith!'"

- **Ned / Jensen Beach, Florida**

A 1995 in-studio interview with the popular CCM group, The Imperials.
(I'm the guy on the right. Try to ignore the mullet.)

My official "coming out" speech at the
2011 Oklahoma Freethought Convention.

At the March 2012 Reason Rally.

*When the religious ask me if I ever truly met Jesus,
I always refer them to this photo.*

A rare gathering of online activists at the 2011 American Atheists Conventio
From left to right: Rob Slockbower (Devchelle2), Peach Braxton, me, DPRJo
AronRa, Ashley Paramore (HealthyAddict), Thunderf00t and Cristina Rac
(ZOMGitCriss).

On stage in Los Angeles with Matt Dillahunty of "The Atheist Experience
and Cara Santa Maria of "The Skeptics' Guide to the Universe."

Carved by William Piore of the Atheist Community of Tulsa, this jack-o-lantern with the TTA logo is just one of countless ways that members of TTA community show their support.

Another avid fan, Stacey, had the TTA "bulb" tattooed on her arm!

Jessica Alhquist, the "Evil Little Thing," was the subject of national news headlines in the Ahlquist VS Cranston court case. She was kind enough to j[ ]me for a photo at the 2012 Ascent of Atheism Convention in Denver, CO.

AronRa, a popular YouTube activist and friend.
(I know what you're thinking. We could be brothers.)

In 2011, The Thinking Atheist community raised over $15,000 for the secular aid organization, Responsible Charity. In a show of gratitude, the recipients of the charity sent a photo of themselves holding my picture. In truth, the thanks goes to the TTA community. They inspire me.

On stage at the Oklahoma Freethought Convention in June of 2012.

I saw this "trophy," a casting of an Australopithecus afarensis skull, on the Richard Dawkins Foundation for Science and Reason table at a conference, and I had to stop for a photo. (Hint: I'm the one on the right.)

One of the great honors of my life, shaking the hand of Richard Dawkins, whose book "The God Delusion" was so instrumental in my own journey out of superstition.

CHAPTER 12
God Glasses

Still reeling with scripture shock, I moved even further from reaction toward pro-action, deciding to officially present my concerns to Christian family members, friends, associates, and even clergy. Was I missing something? How many others out there had been duped? What would the reaction be?

It was as much a social experiment as anything. I struck up conversations. I wrote letters. I joined forums. I attended apologetics conferences. I had long lunches with educated believers. I started random Facebook threads challenging specific scriptures. I lobbed tough questions and absorbed the return volleys.

I kept this up for about a year. It was fascinating. It was excruciating. Day after day, letter after letter, conversation after conversation, I encountered a litany of unimpressive, vague, and often ridiculous explanations from otherwise intelligent people. Some responses were wispy and sweet. Others were defensive and defiant. Some spoke romantically about personal experiences. Others barked the hard catchphrases of apologetics. Many became defensive. (As I sifted through the responses and the personalities behind them, I also found patterns so recognizable and predictable that I eventually placed the personality types into four basic categories: the Feeler, the Theologian, the Folklorist, and the Foot Soldier. I explain these categories in the next chapter).

Time and again, I watched religious people twist science, history, and scientific evidence to pretzel proportions as they responded to my queries. How could Bronze Age humans like Methuselah live to be 900 years old? *Our DNA was purer back then.* Science verifies that a singularity (Big Bang) took place billions of years ago. *So what came before the Big Bang?* Overwhelming evidence reveals that humans and apes have common ancestors . *I didn't evolve from an ape!* Can you explain the violent and barbaric behavior of the God of the Bible? *You have to read it in context.*

It's ironic that so many Christians are against dancing; they do it so well. The ultimate showcase for the theological two-step was the wildly popular Bible story of Noah's ark, which was a happy story of my childhood. Seen with the more objective eye, it comes off like a horror movie.

As a kid, I was told a tale of judgment, yes, but the horrific details were hidden under the happy story of a happy servant rounding up happy animals which gladly marched - two by two – toward a happy ending painted with with blue skies, rainbows, doves, family, and God's promise never to flood the earth again.

Basking in my newfound midlife skepticism, I read the story again, and my cheeks no doubt flushed with embarrassment as the happy ending got washed away with the rotting corpses of every condemned man, woman, teenager, child, infant, fetus, animal and plant. God's Word asserted that they were all evil, including the elderly, the infirmed, the newborn, even the mentally ill. Only Noah and his family would escape with their lives. And God's method for exterminating all life was the world's largest drowning pool.

Once again, my queries began. And once again, the answers that returned were the stuff of sick comedy or macabre horror.

How did a 600-year-old man build a stadium-sized boat with only trees and pitch? Did no one else on earth have a boat? How did Noah fit millions of animal species onto the ark? What about ventilation? Sanitation? Atrophy from the animals' unused muscles? How did the ark remain afloat with the prohibitive weight loads of the world's animals? What about the aquatic creatures outside of the boat that would die from the mixture of salty sea water and fresh rainwater? Why did Noah have to send a dove to find land if he and God were on speaking terms in the earlier verses? Did it even matter if the dove discovered land, as the ark had no sail, no rudder, and no motor…meaning it couldn't have been steered in any case? If the animal and plant life had been wiped out by the flood, what did Noah, his family and all the animals eat? How did Noah and his family repopulate the earth via incest to create 5,000 ethnic groups in just 4,000 years? Does it make sense that the hero of this story, the man deemed worthy and righteous by God, spent his latter days naked and drunk? Why does all peer-reviewed geological evidence refute all notions of a global flood? And why did God have to develop a hugely convoluted Rube Goldberg mechanism for this purification of sin when he could have simply made all the sinners disappear into vapor?

The replies were priceless. And worthless. The faithful stretched and equivocated and wailed and lamented my lack of faith. They bloviated about dinosaur eggs on the ark, archeological findings on various middle eastern mountains, "kinds" of animals versus "species" of animals, and one guy enthusiastically claimed that Arizona's

Grand Canyon was created in a matter of minutes as the earth vomited up flood waters at God's command.

These people had already bought the story hook, line, and sinker. They were approaching it backwards, putting the conclusion first and scrambling to find the evidence to support it. They were looking at everything through God Glasses.

God Glasses do much more than color one's worldview. They filter out uncomfortable incoming rays of light. They numb the senses. They quell curiosity. They turn smiles and frowns into mannequin stares. They turn thinking adults into drones, sheep, slaves...blissfully happy Eloi right out of H.G. Wells.

Here's a typical conversation between a skeptic and a Christian fundamentalist wearing God Glasses:

Q: How do you know that the bible is the word of God?
A: The Bible tells me so.

Q: But why do you believe the Bible is true?
A: Because it's infallible.

Q: How do you know it's infallible?
A: Because it's the word of God.

Ding! And that's our final answer. Thanks for playing!

Apparently, across the globe and by the millions, Christians had declared modern science tainted and suspect while accepting as fact wild scriptural tales of talking donkeys (Numbers 22:27), demon infested pigs (Matthew 8:32), levitation (Acts 1:9), curses (Exodus 7-10), giants (Genesis 6:4), flying chariots of fire (2 Kings 2:11), the walking undead (John 11:44), and supermen who gained strength based on hair length(Judges 16:17).

The religious scoffed at radiometric dating, transitional fossils, the Hubble Constant, macroevolution, beneficial mutations, the geologic column and the bulk of the respected scientific community's established "facts." They rang the alarm bells of conspiracy and warned of Satan's infiltration into the institutes of science. Some spoke wistfully about complexity. Others spoke in nebulous poems about The Quantum (which confused everyone within earshot). They drowned mainstream research in cynicism and skepticism while their own doctrines and dogmas remained high and dry.

Meanwhile, while the platitudes were flying like machine gun bullets, these same gladiators for God contradicted their own assertions at every turn. If they had witnessed a terrible car accident involving a loved one, would they immediately drop to their knees and call down the supreme power of their omnipotent Lord? Of course not! They'd scramble for their cell phones to call 9-1-1 before navigating a gauntlet of ambulance rides, expensive surgeries, human-made medications and prolonged rehabilitation provided by a diligent hospital staff. Oh, sure, the religious would pray, eventually, but only after they had revealed where their trust was truly placed. To them, this scenario made perfect sense.

Everywhere I went, fully-grown religious adults looked at me through God Glasses, reveling in simple, pat, easy-to-swallow, bumper sticker explanations. They were rarely ruffled by a legitimate challenge. They almost never asked questions that weren't rhetorical. They were messengers. They were bullhorns. The religious were a broadcast tower, transmitting platitudes on every frequency with no inbound receiver.

They weren't listening. And they were starting to piss me off.

"In retrospect, I suppose I don't have too many frustrations about my religious upbringing. It has enabled me to think more critically about the whole system because I have been part of it – I know what it is like to be told that God exists, that good people go to Heaven and that bad people go to Hell, and I can now look back and laugh that such a system manages to influence anyone but children."

- **Daniel / Queensland, Australia**

CHAPTER 13
The Dogma Defenders

I'd once been taught that Christianity was The Way and that all other religions were false, deceptions, ridiculous, and wrong. But by 2008, I could no longer separate Christianity from the other faiths, and for the first time, I was struck by the two obvious culprits that determined religious belief: family and geography.

I started to initiate conversations with the religious by asking two simple questions:

1) *Where were you born?*

2) *What is the religion of your parents?*

Time and again, the answers lined up like a row of guilty shoplifters. Born in the American Midwest with Christian parents? *Christian.* Born in Mexico with Catholic parents? *Catholic.* Born in the Middle East to Muslim parents? *Muslim.* Born in Asia to Hindu parents? *Hindu.* And so on.

With the rogue exception, the religions of these men, women, and youths could be directly traced to the religions of generations past and cultures present. All believed that they were enlightened while the rest were deceived. All felt fortunate (blessed?) that they had been raised with The Correct Religion while counterfeit faiths spun towards chaos and oblivion. And all were actively downloading those same religions into the soft skulls of children and grandchildren. Natural curiosity was muted by the hard, fast *CLANK* of the rubber stamp. Charged with populating Paradise, religious parents hadn't been teaching. They had been replicating.

Richard Dawkins had hit the nail on the head in his 2006 book, "The God Delusion," with the assertion that children accept freely the teachings of their parents as fact. My friend Bill Morgan, an apostate who was on the founding staff of Oral Roberts University in the 60s, likened religious indoctrination to installing a program on a child's mental hard drive. Parents write the code and install the software, but their religious program carries no uninstall solution. As with any computer program, the code can be wiped and replaced, but only by outside means, often requiring painstaking effort, and in many instances, the user has no idea the removal option is even there.

Yeah. That's pretty accurate. My parents never gave me the option of disbelief. They were desperate to rescue me from Hell and genuinely wanted to see me enjoy Heaven. They installed the most comprehensive program they could muster and ran it 24/7. My formative years would be lived according to that program, and I would accept it for decades before realizing there might be other options.

Options. What were the options?

As the cloud continued to lift, I browsed the other major religions, but they presented the very same credibility challenges as Christianity, failing all burdens of proof. Beyond that, I was struck by the similarities of the other major religions to Christianity. Each had a divine spirit or deity. Each had sacred texts. Each had rituals.

Each desired to make converts of others. Each promised posthumous existence. Certainly, the window dressing was different, but the central tenets were eerily similar. The religions of the world had cooked up their own signature dishes using the same ingredients. Of course, each claimed enlightenment (these charges often coming from the mouths of high priests in love with the sound of their own voices), but each ultimately shattered under the stress test of science and reason.

Christians, Catholics, Muslims, Mormons, Jehovah's Witnesses, Orthodox Jews, Confucianists, Hindus and equally rabid proponents of countless other faiths were all performing their own, unique, interpretive dance to the very same song. And again, the origins of each person's faith could almost always be traced to the family's religion and geographic location.

As I had started to become numb from the uncritical responses to my Bible-related questions, I was also struck by the style-over-substance defenses of religion. The apologists at every level seemed to fall into patterns as they defended their deities and holy books, prompting me to sort them into four major categories:

1) The Feeler

The Feeler often had a Bible in tow and easily interjected God and Jesus into everyday conversation. The Feeler took great comfort in his Savior, and any inconsistencies or chaos in the world was quickly brushed away with the knowledge that "God is in control." The Feeler was big-hearted but easily flustered. Scientific, philosophical and moral challenges to his faith frustrated him, like an irritating noise that had to be blocked out.

The Feeler was easy prey in any real debate on spiritual issues. If I asked him about the logistics of the Creation argument, his understanding of evolution, the characteristics of the cosmos, or why he chose his deity over another, I rarely got an answer beyond, "I just know it in my heart." He didn't *know* how or why, and by his own admission, he wasn't supposed to know. The Feeler required no proof before purchase, and ignorance was often brandished like a badge of honor, the happy fantasy being far preferable to hard reality.

2) The Theologian

He was educated, erudite and scholarly. In my interactions with a Theologian, he usually prefaced his responses with a long resume, presenting his credentials before delving into thick speech designed to impress and overwhelm.

When I challenged this Christian "expert" on the historical accuracy of scripture, he almost always quoted the Bible. Of course, this would be like quoting the Qur'an to prove the Qur'an, or perhaps quoting Harry Potter to prove Harry Potter.

With wordy diatribes, convoluted analysis, and thick rebukes of the ignorant unwashed, the Theologian excused all manner of biblical atrocity, contradiction and inaccuracy with equivocations about the original manuscripts, the processes of scripture canonization, the best translations, the historical contexts and ancient customs that were required to properly comprehend God's (simple?) message of salvation thousands of years later. He hop-scotched from verse to verse, from chapter to chapter, from Old Testament to New Testament, cross-referencing, explaining local customs, dissecting words in the Greek and Hebrew, using the guidance of the Holy

Spirit to properly convey the meanings in every passage.

And of course, when things got too sticky, too complicated, too incon-venient or too ridiculous, the Theologian would either state that God works in mysterious ways OR exclaim that the story was a metaphor, a parable, an object lesson told in the abstract. (After all, it would be presumptuous to take the scriptures *literally*.)

The Theologian was adept at redirection, answering questions that I never actually asked. If I queried about why God doesn't intervene in tragic situations, I would get several paragraphs about how Eve suc-cumbed to temptation in the Garden of Eden. If I took that bait and asked for evidence of the Creation story, the Theologian would boldly protest that he "didn't come from a monkey." And if I once again took the left turn and pointed to hard evidence of common ancestry, he'd quote from memory 1 Timothy 4:1, "The Spirit clearly says that in lat-er times some will abandon the faith and follow deceiving spirits and things taught by demons."

Superior and condescending, the Theologian uttered lofty words from a high perch, unimpressed by the disagreements of lesser minds. However, Theologians together in a room would clash like bumper cars, colliding over the very basic tenets of their own faiths: Baptism. Eternal security. Heaven. Hell. Prosperity. Healing. Miracles. The sim-plest of subjects was fodder for debate and disagreement, and watching theses high priests square off was entertaining and often comical.

Still, for sheer comic relief, the next category stood far above the others.

3) The Folklorist

The Folklorist had just enough information to make him dangerous.

His antennae was always up, listening for another piece of "proof" that God exists, and then he re-transmitted that information without bothering to fact-check it.

He'd hear a headline about a boat-shaped geological discovery in Turkey and immediately email 50 people, exclaiming that Noah's Ark had been found. Of course, he couldn't be bothered with a simple Google search to discover that the site was actually a natural formation on the earth's crust.

The Folklorist would send photos of the final moments of the World Trade Center, where an image of the devil's face could be seen amidst the exploding ball of flame. ("9/11 was attack by Satan, and here is the proof!") Apparently, the Folklorist had never heard of Photoshop or read neuroscience studies about "patternicity."[7]

Here's a classic example of the Folklorist. Remember back in the 80s and 90s, when Christians boycotted Proctor & Gamble products because the P&G trademark was a sign of Satan? The "man and moon" symbol was declared demonic, and the Folklorist did his Christian duty by warning everyone to boycott. Again, even before the internet, a phone call or trip to the library would have revealed a less shocking truth. The symbol was actually created by a crate maker in the 1800s to help organize dock shipments. P&G grew so tired of the controversy that they eventually changed their emblem.

The Folklorist probably grew up playing his records backwards to find Satanic messages, looking for God-shaped cloud formations, bending everything in the book of Revelation to match the evening news, and projecting divine meaning onto everyday coincidences. ("I ran into Suzie today at Wal-Mart after twenty years. God must

_____

7   http://www.scientificamerican.com/article.cfm?id=patternicity-finding-meaningful-patterns

have brought her into my life for a *reason*.")

In the debate arena, the Folklorist was usually knocked out in the first round, because his claims were so easily refuted. One or two sentences were usually all it took to send him packing, often in an embarrassed and somewhat wounded state.

The Folklorist never actually allowed any of these exchanges to change his mind, however. He simply removed the debunked myth from his list and carried on to the next one. (But he STILL refuses to buy Proctor & Gamble…just in case.)

My final category defined an aggressive and often angry fellow:

THE FOOT SOLDIER

Usually a strong personality, The Foot Soldier attempted to defend God by flipping the discussion 180 degrees.

Not as well-versed as the Theologian, he championed Christianity from the front lines instead of the war room. Legitimate questions were bounced back with righteous indignation.

CHALLENGE: Why did God allow the horror of Germany's Holocaust?
RESPONSE: Miracles happened during the Holocaust! Talk to the survivors! And evil was defeated! Who are you to question God?

CHALLENGE: Why doesn't God simply feed the millions of starving people in the world?
RESPONSE: God uses man. God wants man to be a missionary to the world. God WANTS to save them, but he WANTS to use man. Who are you to question God?

CHALLENGE: Why does God create a physical, tangible creature desperate for answers, and then insist on providing no physical proof of Himself?

RESPONSE: God has proven Himself! He's real! He's in my heart! Who are you to question God?

The Foot Soldier's tactic was to use force to keep the questioner on the defensive. From his perspective, anyone who dared to put Christianity to the fire MUST be delusional, misled or sought to be God himself.

The Foot Soldier loved a good fight, argued with peaked emotion and often trampled over weaker opponents with sheer verve. But the fact that his debate vessel was loud and fast did not mean it was soundly constructed. He was the rusty car with the beefy engine, revving loudly in an attempt to drown out the competitors, and choking everyone in the vicinity with his thick exhaust.

Ultimately, the Feeler, the Theologian, the Folklorist, and the Foot Soldier usually had one thing in common: they were all absolutely convinced. Their varied paths had led them to a destination of subjective certainty. They couldn't prove it, but somehow the un-provability of God made His existence even truer.

My discussions, debates and exchanges with these God Warriors only drove me further away from religion, each lame response or laughable assertion striking my senses like a foul odor. I became more and more convinced that I had been baptized (metaphorically and literally) into a culture that blindfolded its children at birth, housing them in the dark, keeping them dependent, and shackling them with an inherited worldview that reflected their guardians. Without sight, the young, the weak, the impressionable, and the vulnerable could be more easily controlled, kept within established boundaries, and conditioned to fear any scenario where the blinders might come off.

In the late months of 2008, after a navigating the volatile minefield of superstition, tradition, and woo-woo, and after watching science constantly trump religious assertions with minimal effort, I finally verbalized what I'd secretly known for months. God was a phantom. A fairy tale. A myth.

I found no convincing proof for any god, anywhere. Not in my own mind. Not through scripture. Not via any "evidence." And certainly not by the apologist acrobats that couldn't reconcile their claims with the facts or with each other.

I would no longer project human behavior, natural phenomenon, coincidence or luck onto an invisible wizard in the sky. I would no longer give credence to the agents of faith: intuition, assumption, gut feelings, goose bumps, dreams, visions, premonitions, voices, wish thinking, etc. I came to see the church as a prison, the high walls and watch towers hidden by glitzy chandeliers and stained glass, and I had somehow crawled under the wall to freedom, experiencing the liberating and terrifying sensations that came with it.

I was an atheist. And my next thought was (pardon the irony), "Holy shit."

"My roommate asked me, 'So are you saying you don't believe any of it anymore?' After a long pause, I replied, 'Yeah, I guess that's right.' It felt as though a huge burden had lifted."

- **Tony / Syracuse, New York**

CHAPTER 14

Jesus Town

Oklahoma. The epitome of Flyover Country. In the imagination of the outsider, it's the untamed Sooner state, a flat, brown, tumbleweed-littered wheat field populated with cowboys, cattle, oil derricks, and Larry the Cable Guy. (I once had relatives drive down from Minnesota to visit, and they were genuinely expecting teepees on a Gunsmoke-esque vista of horses and wild prairies. They wouldn't walk in the yard for fear of rattlesnakes. No kidding.)

Ranked 28th in population[8] and much lower in several education statistics[9] Oklahoma stands in the shadow of the more densely populated and "progressive" states arrayed on the west and east coasts. My hometown, Tulsa, is often a convenient punch line for the coasts, as seen in the 2002 "Friends" episode where Chandler laments having to spend the holidays there.

I was born in Tulsa and never felt a compulsion to leave. With just under half a million residents, it's a city that's not sprawling or congested. You can buy a two-story house for the cost of an efficiency apartment in Los Angeles. It's clean and well planned. The people are friendly. You can drive the city limits in about thirty minutes. It's

---

8   U.S. Census 2010
9   "2008-09 Facts: Oklahoma Public Schools". Oklahoma State Department of Education. 2010

like Mayberry with interstate highways.

Tulsa doesn't have a big night life, or a major sports team, or popular tourist attractions. But it DOES have two things in abundance: tornados and churches.

The tornados are easier to escape.

In the early days of 2009, I found myself a freshly emerged (and slightly rattled) atheist, liberated from the cocoon of religion, but realizing with increasing alarm that I had suddenly regressed to minority status. I had left the church parade to march to a different tune and ended up a one-man band. And despite the fact that I maintained relationships with my family and friends, I became almost overwhelmed by a sense of isolation. The Bible belt was tightened to the last notch around my social circle.

God-speak was everywhere. *Praise Jesus. God bless you. I'll pray for you. God is so good. Thank you, Lord, for this meal. Thank God for this beautiful weather. God is my co-pilot. God bless Oklahoma. God bless America. God bless us, everyone.* For the first time in my life, I found these saccharine platitudes empty, sad, often disgusting, as they almost always ignored human accomplishment in favor of a fairy godfather. My former brethren sounded like a Mentos commercial, spewing sugary clichés that would make many politicians retch. These were not environments for meaningful personal connection, especially if I was looking for support on my new path of non-belief.

I was an apostate in Jesus Town, and I needed support. For me (and many others I've met in the days since), apostasy was like dealing with the death of a familiar friend, complete with accompanying stages of grief: shock, denial, pain, anger, depression, acceptance, and (in my case, anyway) satisfaction. Yet even as I was discovering a bigger, better world beyond Christianity, I was being pinged constantly by well-meaning loved ones desperate to bring the prodigal son home again.

It was my mother on the telephone when I first announced that I was an atheist. She immediately corrected me, "No. You're not an atheist. You just have questions. You're just going through a difficult time. Doubts are natural. It'll be OK. You'll come to see the truth. But you're not an atheist." I insisted that the label was accurate and that I was an absolute non-believer, but she would not be convinced. She was obviously blinking away the unthinkable notion that her son's outright rejection of Yahweh would sentence him to a painful, fiery, eternal Hell.

That phone call soon digressed into a raw display of desperation, emotion bleeding through my mother's voice. She protested. She argued. She wept.

If I may digress for a moment, I must say that there are few experiences like hearing a mother weep over her child's condemned eternal soul and knowing that, aside from lying to yourself and others, there's nothing you can do to ease her pain. For me, those tears alone are reason enough to despise religion and seek its destruction, as its claims have so heinously grieved a mother and father in regard to their son. A ridiculous book of myths written by anonymous primitives has absolutely convinced my parents of God and the devil, of angels and demons, of miracles and curses, of Heaven and Hell, and now they must somehow reconcile the notion that their omniscient, omnipotent, just, and loving deity will soon toss their beloved child into the torture chamber.

Adding insult to my claim of apostasy was the fact that both of my parents are bible scholars who have dedicated the larger portion of their lives to teaching, preaching, and promoting Christianity. Their bookshelves are lined with scripture study guides, books on biblical prophecy, and an impressive assortment of apologist ammunition. Decades ago, my mother wrote a Greek New Testament study guide used at the college level, and she wrote sermons for pastors who had once attended her Greek study courses. Married in 1967, my parents honeymooned in the Holy Lands, spending their first days as husband and wife walking the shores of Galilee and the streets of Jerusalem. At one point in his life, my father dedicated his efforts toward memorizing the Book of Revelation. The entire book.

Yeah. My parents weren't pretenders. They weren't Sunday Christians. They were (and remain) the genuine article. The lifelong love they showered on their children was only eclipsed by their desire for each of us to have a personal relationship with Jesus Christ, avoid the snares of the devil, and ultimately rendezvous with everyone on the family tree at the pearly gates to enjoy an eternity in Heaven.

Yet somehow, despite all their efforts (and to their absolute horror), a child had been tainted by the wiles of Beelzebub, uprooting the very faith seeds they'd so carefully planted and nurtured. It was a slap in the face. It was humiliating. It was maddening. It was the worst-case scenario. And it had to be stopped.

By early 2009, the volume of email exchanges intensified. My parents simply couldn't rest until I had been brought back into the fold, so they launched a strategic assault from multiple angles. One day I'd be given "facts" about "science" which "proved" Creationism. Later, I'd be chided for blindly believing anything spoken or written by Richard Dawkins, the pied piper of atheism. Subsequent emails would trod out the tired, hackneyed arguments about morality, the science conspiracy against God, the evidence for Noah's flood and Jesus' existence, the notion that belief in evolution is atheistic, the Second Law of Thermodynamics, Hitler, irreducible complexity, etc. And I would oblige each advance with a return volley of rebuttals and appropriate sources.

Those types of exchanges went on for a long period of months, and their incessant crossing of boundaries ultimately sabotaged our relationship. Those incessant emails and long phone conversations only cultivated a feeling of isolation and separation within me, and even the most innocuous holiday gatherings or family reunions were overshadowed by this dark cloud of division. Just past the smiles and hugs and small talk stood the elephant in the room, the uneasy beast threatening to stampede at the slightest provocation. Often, at the end of those gatherings, I'd be given a book to read, a totem of spiritual enlightenment which would undoubtedly help me understand and accept the love of God.

I remember one occasion when, after a pleasant lunch with my parents, we walked to the parking lot and my mother retrieved a book from her car. Proudly handing it to me, she said, "Read this." It was Alister McGrath's "The Dawkins Delusion? Atheist Fundamentalism and the Denial of the Divine." I calmly asked what the gist of the book's argument was, and my mother shrugged and admitted that she hadn't read it. For her, it was enough that McGrath's book was anti-Dawkins, and no further examination of the text was necessary.

Take note. This is how the religious approach a great many things.

Compounding the overall tension was the fact that I had recently hit an ominous age milestone (40), and I'm sure there were plenty of concerned prayer warriors convinced that my hard U-turn away from God was simply part of the midlife crisis that would also eventually manifest itself through designer clothes, a motorcycle, dancing lessons, a trophy girlfriend, hair plugs, and a long camping excursion in the mountains so that I could *find myself.*

Yes, this crisis of the spirit was allegedly "just a phase" that would work itself out. Eventually.

Amplifying that perception was the very real fact that my personal life was in shambles, and I was on the final leg of an 18 year marriage. Those were very dark days, as two people had transformed from lovers to friends to mere roommates. It is the time in my life of which I am the least proud, as I was disconnected, unpleasant, and completely uninterested in reconciliation. While my wife sought (Christian) counseling and potential recovery of the union, I remained passive and mute, already mentally packing my bags. And even though this was the same time period where I felt tremendous dissatisfaction with my once-cherished religion, I cannot blame the dissolution of our marriage on religious issues. The subject of God certainly added fuel to the fire, but the spark of division had ignited years before.

Fortunately, the divorce was amicable, and my ex-wife and I have since restored and cultivated a friendship that I am tremendously thankful for. We've taken a hard, forensic look at the circumstances which led to the breakup, and we've decided that friendship was what we were always best at. So, friends we remain. For this, I am profoundly grateful.

Those around me did not share my gratitude. At the time, I was the only person in my immediate family to have been divorced, and this fact undoubtedly prompted another point deduction. In their eyes, I was a failure spiritually AND relationally, a midlife meltdown, a cautionary tale told in whispers.

When I interacted with my parents, I couldn't help but hear that nauseating tone of pity and condescension that so often oozes from the mouths of the morally superior. Their words were pleasant, but their tone was forced and dripping with disappointment. They couldn't understand me. They couldn't relate to me. They couldn't fix me. How had this apple fallen so far from the tree?

So there I was…the bad apple, the Oklahoma son of theologian parents, an infidel in the Bible belt, feeling more alone than at any time in my life. Nobody was listening. Nobody understood. Nobody could relate. And while churches around me enjoyed the bonds of community and support, I was isolated and alone. I had no community.

So, I decided to build one.

*"I no longer pray for things to improve.
I work to improve them myself."*

-     **Ted / Texas**

CHAPTER 15
The Thinking Atheist

One by-product of the previous year's quest for answers was the small mountain of notes, emails, reference materials, Bible verses and personal journal entries I had compiled in my quest for information. By early 2009, I'd run the apologetics gauntlet and emerged with a pretty good idea of where the major traps were. In fact, I was beginning to hear so many of the same pro-God arguments that I could reflexively locate most of the appropriate refutations in my stack within a few minutes. The impossibility of Noah's ark? Contradicting scriptural accounts of Christ's crucifixion, resurrection and ascension? Sadistic edicts from a jealous deity? Evidence for the Big Bang, common ancestry and Evolution by Natural Selection? Arguments from emotion or personal experience? I simply flipped to the corresponding point in my makeshift rolodex or popped off the counter-argument from memory.

As a result of this compilation (and also because I was desperate to reach beyond the happy-clappy church culture all around me), I decided to design a website, create an online community and begin producing atheism-related videos. My previous searches for online material had been fruitful, but I found myself frustrated by the clinical and unintuitive layouts. Navigating these atheist websites was often like combing through stereo instructions. The information was there, but tucked away behind lists and links and long (very long!) paragraphs of black text on plain white backgrounds. Locating specific information was often like finding a needle in a stack of needles, and I imagined many page visitors giving up and moving on.

In 2009, before the quality bar was significantly raised by activists worldwide, atheist video material on the internet was even more frustrating. The content was solid, but the producers obviously had no idea where to place the camera, how to mic the subject(s), when and how to use music, graphics, and production elements, etc. They placed inadequate cameras on the back walls of lecture halls, reducing the subject to a tiny blip existing beyond a room full of heads. The videographers often forgot to white-balance their cameras (Google it), and the resulting final product sometimes gave the lecturer green hair or orange skin. Intro music often sounded like it came from an 80s-era video game.

Don't misunderstand. These people were working with what they had, almost certainly donating their time to record and upload these events to benefit the cause of free thought. For this, I am genuinely grateful. But regardless of the noble intentions of the producers, a large portion of these recorded lectures, short-form features, and podcasts fell flat. They lacked the single and most critical element: storytelling.

I must explain that, as a radio announcer and video producer, I have a passion for storytelling. Probably to a fault, I find myself anxious to tell stories, both fact and fiction, in ways that are most palatable and compelling to the widest possible audience. In my opinion, effective storytelling requires efficiency, momentum, timing, good instincts, and something that, in my old radio days, we used to call a *relate*.

A *relate* is anything that creates an environment of empathy in the audience. If you share an anecdote about the time you locked your keys in your car (while it was running), or had a loved one surprise you on your birthday, or had to replace a cherished piece of furniture after the cat turned it into a scratching post, you're *relating* a story that rings bells of familiarity in the mind of whoever is listening. Even in fiction, audiences are most connected to the material when they can relate to certain characteristics of the players, whether physical, intellectual, or emotional. The best stories are the ones that people take personally, and the *relate* can be enhanced with language, lighting, camera angle, soundtrack, etc.

Here's a great example of the make-or-break consequences of bad storytelling. A huge fan of the NASA and U.S. space program, I'm a sucker for any documentary on the Gemini missions, the Apollo program, Neil Armstrong's giant leap for mankind, the shuttle flights, the space station, etc. It's staggering to imagine human explorers strapped to highly explosive rockets, lunging skyward to escape the grasp of the earth's gravity and ultimately spin around the planet at over 17,000 miles per hour.

Motivation. Danger. Fear. Ambition. Exhilaration. Courage. Wonder. Awe. Accomplishment. Joy. These are elements that almost all humans can relate to, and wrapped in the context of manned space flight, they color some of the most amazing stories in human history.

So what's one of the most sterile, bland, and least viewed channels on television? The NASA channel.

Populated with dry mission footage, monotone press conferences, and lackluster post-production, the NASA channel is (in my humble opinion) lousy at telling its own story. For the compelling productions and engaging storytelling our space program deserves, you instead must switch over to Discovery, The Science Channel or NatGeo. Yes, NASA's tale is often better told by someone else

I personally felt that the atheist community had a storytelling problem. We had a few gems like Richard Dawkins' 2007 documentary, "The Enemies of Reason" and Bill Maher's "Religulous," but the lion's share of atheist-related material was…meh. And I wondered if I, as a professional video producer and storyteller, might have anything to contribute to the cause.

I hope that assertion doesn't come across as haughty or egotistical. There are many, many skills I do not possess. I can barely change the oil in my car. I can't draw or paint. I'm cannot sing. I have zero athleticism. I'm a lousy dancer. And I have the memory of a goldfish. BUT! Through audio, video, or spoken word, I know how to tell a story, and after my own long, messy, and ultimately empowering journey out of religion, I was convinced that I had something to offer.

So, my mission became to organize and ultimately translate the most digestible arguments against my former religion into a navigable website and professionally-produced videos, making those elements compelling, fun and, relatable. Admittedly, it would be a relatively shallow dip in the vast waters of counter-apologetics. I'm no genius, but I have had a long, clear view of the Christian culture and can speak to it with authority. I was cradled in the embrace of Christianity from my earliest memories. I was educated in a religious school. I stood on stages, spoke from podiums, and fashioned years of radio shows around my faith. Personally and professionally, I had witnessed, literally, hundreds of church services across the country, and as a storyteller, I had the ability and opportunity to examine and explain my former religion with an intimate, inside-out perspective.

My new website would become a conduit, a channel where I could connect with other non-believers, vent my own frustrations as a new apostate, have some fun and, just maybe, encourage and empower others on their own difficult journeys. I wanted the site to be simple, attractive, populated with basic yet relevant content and, ultimately, to sound the charge for others to cast off the inherited worldviews of their families and cultures. My unofficial coda was, *Assume nothing. Question everything. And start thinking.*

On April 13, 2009, I secured my website domain: **www.thethinkingatheist.com**

When I created The Thinking Atheist (TTA) brand and logo, I most definitely was not attempting to position myself as the thinking atheist. TTA was a symbol, an icon, an encouragement to reject faith and embrace reason.

In my own life, I harbored guilt and shame that I had spent so many years blindly swallowing information spoon-fed to me by parents, pastors and religious "experts." When the Bible got messy or my questions became too inconvenient, I was encouraged by many Christians to disengage my brain. They'd flash that smug smile and tell me, "You're thinking too much. You need to let the spirit guide you. You need to take it on faith."

Indeed. Faith was the drug that dulled the mind, glazed the eyes, and pacified the uneasy conscience. Faith cured all ills, explained all mysteries, and won all arguments. It was the ultimate get-out-of-thinking-free card. Having faith was considered wonderful, something to be proud of.

Of course, now I perceive such notions about faith much differently. I conducted an interview with a young man named William for my September, 2012 video titled "Farewell to Faith," and he summed up the issue perfectly. He said, "I feel like, when people say (sic) 'I'm a man of faith,' they should be ashamed as opposed to proud of it. It's like driving with your eyes closed."

Absolutely. Faith isn't a virtue. It's a cop out. It's an excuse for laziness. Faith encourages otherwise skeptical people to shrug, to assume, to accept. People of faith take license to avoid any real examination of history, church doctrine, scripture, and the more satisfying conclusions that good science provides. And while these people would never take on faith the other, less critical decisions in their lives (buying a car, choosing a doctor, finding a good school, evaluating a career, planning a financial investment, etc), faith works just fine on matters of eternal destiny.

The religious often assert that the secular person is just as guilty of having faith. They counter with challenges like, "How do you know the sun will rise tomorrow? You take it on faith!" Actually, the secular person examines the documented rotation of the earth in relation to the sun and the 4.7 billion years of previous sunrises, and then he/she draws a conclusion based on the evidence. Can the atheist prove absolutely that the sun will rise tomorrow? Nope. But after examining the evidence, I wouldn't bet against it.

And these scenarios dodge the larger question. If God created human beings with natural curiosity and the ability to reason, why would he then make himself undetectable to the curious and reasonable mind? Why the parlor tricks? Why the unverifiable "appearances" or "miracles?" If Heaven and Hell are at stake, why would a just and loving Father make himself impossible to see, hear, smell, touch, and verify? And why would anyone seeking evidence for God be chastised for engaging a God-given brain?

In my newfound freedom from religion, I wanted to remind anyone visiting the website that it was OK, even imperative, to engage critical thought and to demand more satisfying answers than "The Lord works in mysterious ways." Thinking would be endorsed, encouraged, celebrated.

The TTA icon, an outline of a genderless head containing a light bulb, wasn't going to win any design awards. But it was clean, pleasant and easily identifiable. (In 2010, that logo evolved a bit, enhancing the light bulb with a blue supernova and incorporating the atheist "A" symbol.)

Upon its launch in May of 2009, the site was pleasant to look at but – given my limited website knowledge - admittedly basic and amateur. It wasn't very interactive, although the site did provide a forum for those who might want to connect and exchange ideas. The home page had a window that integrated my first-ever atheist video, embedded from the brand new TTA YouTube page, titled "The Invisible God."

"The Invisible God" integrated some basic motion graphics and titles over a cinematic soundtrack. This two-minute video wasn't groundbreaking from a production standpoint, but for me, it was a gigantic step. It was the first time I had ever used my talents as a producer to challenge and ridicule Christianity instead of extolling it. That video – and the newly published website – was an official declaration of war on my former faith. Posting it in such a public place was both exhilarating and terrifying.

I wasn't completely "out" in regards to TTA. I was working anonymously behind the TTA icon, not revealing my name, face, or any personal information. In my day job as video producer, I was still heavily immersed in church-related work and figuring out how to extricate myself. It was a catch-22. A solid editor and good communicator, I'd become a sought-after asset to serve our church clientele, often giving public presentations at religious conferences and workshops. The more I came to reject religion, the more I realized the depth of the hole I was in. How could I effectively serve my employer AND be true to my own personal convictions?

I'd lie awake at night, racked with conflict. I feared that I might be personally and/or professionally punished for my nonbelief. I feared that church-related clients would discover that their producer was actually a double agent. I feared that I might be too inconvenient for my employer (or any employer in this deeply religious city) to keep around. I feared becoming jobless at midlife and suddenly finding myself unable to pay the mortgage, buy the groceries, cover the utility expenses and provide security for my loved ones. I feared the backlash from my religious parents, as they would undoubtedly consider my atheist website the ultimate slap in the face. I also feared that some crazed zealot might one day find my home address and put my family in danger.

I feared a great many things.

Yet I was compelled to keep going. I couldn't wait to finish the workday, bury myself in my home studio and tackle the next atheist video project. It was a compulsion, an addiction, a liberation exercise that made all potential consequences fade into the background. There was a driving force within me, a flame of enthusiasm far beyond anything I had ever experienced in any church revival service.

It was ebullience. It was freedom. It was the sensation of finally finding my own voice, living in my own skin, and desiring to help others to do the same.

This compulsion would intensify over the coming months as one TTA video became two, two became four, four became a dozen. My portfolio was expanding. I was pouring copious amounts of free time (and every spare dollar) into the mission, and eventually the one-two punch of the website and YouTube page started to make a few ripples in the online ocean. A YouTube user would give a positive review in the comments section, or I'd receive a random email from someone who appreciated the forum or the resource page. TTA website analytics would reveal a few hundred (gasp!) visitors in a single month, and I'd find myself smiling.

The Thinking Atheist was the epitome of "grass roots," built by a guy in his home office, and funded with whatever remained in a checking account after the bills got paid. It was my post-religion therapy. It was a labor of love. It was my baby. It gave me joy. It gave me peace.

It gave my family a migraine.

"My kids, now young adults, have thanked me for NOT raising them with religion."

- **Janet / Alaska**

CHAPTER 16
Activism

The second video I produced ultimately became one of TTA's most popular. Titled "The Story of Suzie," the satiric cartoon was my rather clumsy attempt at 2D animation. Truthfully, it wasn't animation at all, merely some character images with keyframes added for motion. Suzie's lips never moved, her limbs only pivoted at the joints, and she could only face one direction in any scene. True animators will undoubtedly cringe at this amateur effort.

But there was something special about "The Story of Suzie," which almost immediately racked up tens of thousands of online views. A teasing look at a fresh young Christian woman seeing the world through her God Glasses, the video was fun, briskly paced, and it drew a suspiciously accurate caricature of religious thinking. The Suzie video would remain a fan favorite, prompting me to give it a graphical facelift eighteen months later. On January 21, 2011, the clip was featured in an article by The Christian Post under the heading, "Atheist Depicts Christians as Delusional in 'Story of Suzie' Video."[10]

(Of course, the Post reporter found plenty of time to interview a

---

10   http://www.christianpost.com/article/20110121/atheist-depicts-christians-as-delusional-in-story-of-suzie-video/

Christian apologist for the story, but she was somehow unable to get in touch with me before publishing the piece. Imagine.)

Yes, The Thinking Atheist was starting to get noticed, with viewer statistics climbing every month. And as the beast began to grow out of infancy, it wasn't long before TTA was on the radar of my family. I became aware of this through the grapevine.

Yet all remained silent. Nobody dialed my cell phone and yelled, "How could you do this?" Nobody sent me long emails lamenting the shame of it all. Nobody knocked on my door and demanded that I immediately cease and desist. In fact, I overheard only the random whisper. The silence was palpable.

It's important you know that I get no joy in watching two wonderful, loving parents heartbroken over my apostasy. It hurts to know that my mom and dad, in the winter of their lives, will spend their remaining years punishing themselves for failing to effectively train up their child in the way that he should go (although I can't imagine what more they might have done). And I realize that my foray into full-blown atheist activism must seem the worst kind of betrayal, TTA flashing like a huge marquee with the words "Our son is repaying his parents for decades of sacrifice by betraying the dreams they held for him."

This is not my desire. Their grief is an unfortunate consequence of a larger goal: to counter the childhood indoctrination, the false teachings, the bad science, and other harmful effects of superstitious thinking.

Across the planet, often well-meaning and sincere mothers and fathers are doing what my parents did; they're fitting their children with intellectual restraints, stifling their natural curiosity, and preconditioning them to be satisfied with the pat answers provided by religion.

Along with talk of faith and bliss, religious parents are also cultivating guilt, shame, and fear. As a result, many of these children spend the rest of their lives chained to the obscene notion that they're broken, tainted, and unworthy, constantly apologizing for being born a sinner, and scrambling to escape punishment by pledging eternal allegiance to an invisible wizard and his book of spells. Even those showered with saccharine assurances that they are precious children of God still often wrestle with important issues relating to life, death, worth, and identity.

Worse yet, the wares of religion aren't just being sold to children. Religion is pitched to young and old in every walk of life. It targets with extreme prejudice the ignorant, the vulnerable, and the wounded, promising respite and comfort to all who sign up. It's a propaganda machine blasting a single message: Accept this gift, or else.

And with great regularity, these religious messages are propagated with the best of intentions. Parents genuinely wish to protect their children from the wiles of Satan. Friends genuinely want the assurance that they'll see each other in Paradise. Pastors genuinely seek to better their communities. Missionaries sincerely desire to feed the hungry, help the sick, build homes (and churches), and rescue the unsaved from Hell. A great, great many champions of faith are operating from a position of absolute sincerity.

Of course, none of these good intentions negates the hard reality of the damage done, and even in TTA's first few months, I received many long and gut-wrenching emails from ex-believers trying to heal from the psychological wounds inflicted upon them for their apostasy. Some were called evil by their own families. Some were kicked out of their homes. Some saw their marriages spiral into bitter divorces. Some had their parents withdraw all financial support for their college educations. Some lost lifelong "friends." And some, accepted only on the surface, still navigated an oppressive undercurrent of resentment and judgment.

Many who wrote to me were still believers who toed the religious line publicly but secretly wrestled with skepticism and doubt, often reaching out under pseudonyms or with signatures of "Anonymous." Their letters often started with lines like, "I'm in a really bad place, and I was hoping you could help."

With each letter, I grew more confident that, despite the difficulties that TTA threatened to cause in my personal life, I was doing the right thing.

Lest you think I harbored a rather noble view of myself, I must admit that my newfound activism was propelled as much by guilt as anything else. I felt guilty (and a bit thick) for taking so long to come to my senses. I felt guilty for all of the times I promoted superstition in a classroom, through a radio microphone, from a podium, wherever. For decades, I had been a part of the problem. TTA was a passion, but it was also restitution for wrongdoing. As a former religious addict, activism was part of my recovery, and I had become a counselor to help others beat the addiction as well.

I wasn't blind enough to think all of this wouldn't sting those on my family tree, but I was also determined not to be emotionally blackmailed into silence ("Why can't you just keep your atheism to yourself? You're embarrassing us!").

I realized that my life belonged to no one else, that my voice shouldn't be a mere echo of another, and that I wouldn't bend to the double standard of the free-speaking religious who acted like they were the only ones with a right to be heard

Ultimately, The Thinking Atheist wasn't and isn't about my family. Its content is not designed to help or hurt them. It's not targeted to them. It's not a tell-all about them. It operates completely separate from them. TTA is about me and people like me. It's for atheists and those curious about atheism. It's a place to exchange information. It's a community. It's therapy. If my parents never click a link or watch a video, if they never visit the Facebook page or view a speech, if they're never swayed from their own religious convictions and remain faithful to the end, I'll be just fine with that.

I love and truly appreciate my family, and while this issue is a difficult divide between us, we're all big kids who should be able to abide disagreements, live in our own skins, and celebrate the many wonderful aspects of our relationship that have nothing to do with religion.

One can at least dream.

*"We can have different opinions,
but we can't have different facts."*

-   **Benny / New York**

CHAPTER 17
Out of the Closet

Holding an atheist convention in Tulsa, Oklahoma is not unlike holding a chess tournament inside a cattle barn. Sure, you could DO it, but is it really the best idea?

This was my first thought when I was invited to be part of the lineup at the Oklahoma Freethought Convention, scheduled for July 30, 2011, and featuring a full-day of secular speakers. Organized by the Atheist Community of Tulsa, it would be held at the All Souls Unitarian Church and would be the first event of its kind in a church-saturated region.

Two years after the website launched, it would also be the first time I showed my face.

I agreed to speak. It would be my official "coming out" as an atheist.

The implications were significant, as the cat would officially be out of the bag. My atheist, infidel, heathen, godless face would be seen by hundreds of attendees and tens of thousands of YouTube viewers. Every relative, every friend, every business associate, and every radio listener who once knew me as a Christian broadcaster would see how far the apple had fallen from the tree. Would I receive angry phone calls from shamed relatives? Would KXOJ listeners stuff my email inbox with scriptures and prayers in an attempt to rescue me? Would my employer decide that I was a black eye on the face of the company? Would there be consequences I hadn't yet considered?

Those outside of devoutly religious cultures must wonder what all of the angst was about. But those *inside* religious cultures know exactly what I was going through. "Atheist" is a word that can rip apart family bonds. It can terminate friendships. It can end careers. It can (and this is not an exaggeration) ruin lives.

How much was I willing to put on the line? How far was I willing to go? And would I someday look back on all of this and lament that I had screwed up my entire life?

I know. It sounds dramatic. But for me, the decision to "come out" was the stuff of many sleepless nights. As I lay in bed staring at the ceiling, I became two people punching at the issue like sparring partners in the ring. *C'mon Seth. You're an atheist.* **Yeah, but this isn't just about a personal non-belief. This is about publicly challenging the sacred cows of religion in my own backyard.** *This is what you wanted. To stir the pot, to shed the light of scrutiny on Christianity, to get people thinking.* **But what about my job? If our church clients find out, they'll freak.** *You're just one guy, not the whole company. And you have the right to be non-religious in your private life.* **Sure. But if I'm cut off, demoted or fired, my "principles" will have punished everyone under my roof.** *You can't be fired for being an atheist. It's illegal!* **But what if my employer found a reason, an excuse to give me the boot?** *They're good people. They're honorable people. You know them. They're better than that.* **But what if the worst-case scenario came true? What if I lost everything? Where would I go? What would I do?**

Am I really ready to risk it all?

I must stop here and say something important about my employ-ers of the time. To their credit (and my relief), they have stood by my constitutionally-protected right to own and profess my personal worldview. Despite our disagreements on religious issues, I was not ostracized, penalized, ridiculed, or treated unfairly in any way by the owner, who fairly declared that I had a Constitutional right to be non-religious as much as any other employee might have a right to be a God-believer.

How did I win this particular lottery? Your guess is as good as mine. But for the understanding and support my company extended to-ward me during that time, I remain tremendously grateful.

Of course, I'm sure that all of my religious associates, personal and professional, would have preferred that I was less bold, less loud, less public about my atheism. And the Oklahoma Freethought Convention would be *very* public.

I would share the stage with an eclectic group of speakers, including two activists who had also found a loyal audience on the internet and would soon become my friends: AronRa and Matt Dillahunty.

I was scheduled in the #3 slot, smack-dab in the middle of the con-ference. I vividly remember the odd sensations of that day.

Firstly, although I was somewhat familiar with the inclusive nature of the Unitarians, I still found it ironic that this anti-religion event was being held in a church. Few things are as surreal as watching attendees wearing "A" lapel pins and "Godless" t-shirts file into a church sanctuary and plant themselves onto hard, wooden church pews (complete with hymnals).

Founded in 1921, All Souls Unitarian Church also lagged behind the technological curve. The sound system was merely adequate. The projection screen hung directly in front of a huge, uncovered window, with sunlight washing out the PowerPoint images. The stage was obviously designed for sermons, and the large, white, formal-looking podium gave the proceedings an awkwardly religious vibe whenever anyone stood behind it.

But I also remember the electricity of the day. Enthusiasm was palpable. Over 300 people packed themselves into the sanctuary with smiles on their faces and genuine excitement in their voices, obviously delighted that an atheist gathering had popped up in the middle of Jesus Town. Inside those walls, non-believers weren't misunderstood, maligned, or ostracized. Nobody snorted condescending platitudes at them or labeled them baby-eating devil worshippers. This was (finally!) a freethought event tailor-made for the skeptic, the non-religious, the atheist. And as each ticket holder entered the building, there was (if you'll forgive my romanticism) a feeling of coming home.

Moments before my introduction, I thought my heart was going to explode. A lifetime of public speaking could not adequately prepare me for the moment I would appear before a standing-room-only crowd, loudly reject the existence of God and essentially apologize for over three decades of having my head up my ass. How would the audience react? Would they respond to my prepared speech? Would my sense of humor translate? Would people be checking their watches and taking suspiciously long bathroom breaks? Would I be heckled? Would the audience connect with me, engage with me, take the journey with me?

I needn't have worried. The second I walked up on stage and looked out at the sea of smiling faces, all nervousness vanished. Those people were everything a speaker could ask for in an audience, responding to my prompts, laughing at my jokes, and displaying a measure of goodwill I had rarely seen, even inside churches. It's like they could read my mind (or at least my face), sensing the early jitters and collectively assuring me, "Hey. It's fine. You're doing great. Keep going!"

I say this without hyperbole: Those forty-five minutes on stage at the Oklahoma Freethought Convention were some of the most gratifying of my entire life, and as I finished the speech with a heartfelt "Thank you," the audience sprung to its feet and gave me an ovation I will never forget. Not ever.

Throughout the day, people approached me with words of gratitude for the website, for my videos, for providing an online community where they could act and interact without fear. Parents introduced me to their kids. People accosted me with bear hugs. Many even asked for autographs (one guy even requesting a signature in his Bible).

I so wish that the religious could have peeked into the windows on that day. They wouldn't have seen the caricatures of non-belief they so often mocked and feared. They wouldn't have witnessed long faces full of sadness or rage. They would have seen wonderful, intelligent, enthusiastic, reasonable, real people who hadn't just come together to expose superstitious thinking. These people had come together to enjoy community, to connect, to support each other. They exuded real joy in their deity-free lives, genuinely thankful to be alive at a time when science is advancing leaps and bounds in its quest for answers.

That day was a milestone in my life. As of July 30, 2011 at 1pm Central time, I was out of the atheist closet.

The cat was indeed out of the bag.

"When I listen to your show, I feel like I am listening to a friend. I feel like someone finally understands."

- **Laura / Sanford, North Carolina**

CHAPTER 18
The Return to Radio

I got my first radio job in 1990.

Back then, broadcasting was an exclusive and often prohibitively expensive start-up venture. Radio studios were loaded with tons of bulky equipment purchased at intimidating prices for anyone wishing to enter the game.

A scenario for starting a new radio station might look like this: Two Studer CD players costing $3,000. Three cart (tape) decks at $1,200 a pop. A Neumann microphone and Symetrix vocal processor might run another $2,200. Add another $15,000 for an Arrakis 15-channel sound console, plus the cost of cables and accessories. The actual radio transmitter could easily top $100K, plus the cost of the radio tower itself and the electricity to broadcast the signal.

Of course, no radio show could ever be broadcast without the appropriate approvals and licenses from the Federal Communications Commission (FCC), which were difficult to get and placed limits on the power of your signal and the area(s) of coverage. And to be a "radio announcer," you had to apply for something called an Operator's License (which meant mailing in an application and a modest fee).

I've vastly oversimplified things here, but I'm trying to draw a broad picture of how the game worked. From talk formats to music formats, the radio landscape was comprised of a few stations with a few announcers run by a few families or corporations. It was too complicated, too exclusive, and too expensive for the civilian to jump in and build stations or shows on his/her own. Besides, the available frequencies had long been taken, so you wouldn't be building a new station as much as buying and converting an existing one, another long and expensive endeavor.

The business gradually loosened up a bit, but radio remained a private club, and you couldn't participate unless you were a member.

And then the internet changed everything.

I left my last full-time radio job in 2004. But (and every radio announcer will tell you this), broadcasting gets into your blood. No matter how brutal the competition, no matter how meager the salary, no matter how intense the inevitable burnout, radio becomes a part of you. It's a bully pulpit for the opinionated. It's a blank page for the storyteller. It's a circus for the clown. It's a theater for the mind. Radio is a landing zone for people who aren't content to have their voices heard organically, but instead feel compelled to blast their alerts, rants, stories, jokes, and/or antics through the loudest possible bullhorn. (When people ask me if radio announcers are motivated by insecurity, insanity, or ego, I always reply, "Yes!")

For many years, morning radio was my life. It was often fulfilling and gratifying, but it wasn't easy. Morning radio is an obstacle course, each day presenting a fresh challenge to attract new listeners, hold existing listeners, and steal other listeners from competitors. Poor ratings can mean a quick demotion or a pink slip. You're surrounded by co-workers who are convinced they're better qualified to sit in your chair. Corporate consultants lurk in the shadows, eager to make "helpful" suggestions and justify their own salaries. Corporations buy and sell radio stations like used cars, each transaction placing your next paycheck on the bubble. And if you survive the business for any length of time, the pre-dawn alarm clocks and ratings rat race often render you weary, cynical, or just numb.

It takes a certain kind of person to do radio. Sometimes you love the game. Sometimes you hate it. Sometimes both.

Radio scratched a creative itch within me. It gave me the opportunity to communicate, to tell stories, to create elaborate productions and to test my wits on the fly. Radio also created opportunities for me to meet people I'd never otherwise meet, travel to destinations I'd never otherwise see, and do things I would never otherwise do. In my radio career, I've flown in a B-17 bomber (in the gun turret!), done charity work in Guatemala and Bolivia, judged a local talent competition for American Idol, and toured New York for album promotions. (I also remember hosting many dozens of much-less-glamorous broadcasts from car dealerships, barbeque joints, clothing stores, skating rinks, gas stations, church fundraisers, and even chiropractic offices.)

When I walked away from radio to become a full-time video producer, I knew it was the right decision. I also accepted the fact that I would never again enjoy connecting with listeners in their homes, cars, workplaces, at concerts, etc. I was no longer a broadcaster. That season had passed.

Then, on July 22, 2010, I was an invited guest on an internet podcast called "The God Discussion."

At that time, you could have fit my knowledge of internet radio in a thimble and still had plenty of room for some Johnnie Walker. *What's a podcast? Radio without a radio station? Hosted out of people's homes? Really???*

That evening, I joined a lineup of other internet activists, and my segment was a basic recounting of my own journey. I called into the show on my cell phone and listened to the other guests on my laptop. It was a positive, even exhilarating experience that, just a few years earlier, would have been technologically unfeasible.

Here was a grass-roots organization that was doing a complete runaround of standard (and expensive) AM/FM radio outlets, instead producing home-grown interview shows for just a few bucks.

I hadn't ever considered such a thing was possible, and it wasn't long before I was exploring ways to add a podcast to The Thinking Atheist online content.

Of course, podcasting has its downsides. In 2010, as I feverishly navigated a mountain of various internet podcasts in an attempt to familiarize myself with the landscape, I was again struck by the dearth of quality. While the bargain-basement production values of some shows made them charming and accessible, many other podcasts sounded like someone had buried a hidden microphone under a sofa at a frat party. Crap audio. Weak content. Forced laughter. Lots of swearing. Unintelligible crosstalk. Awkward silences. Nearly unlistenable.

Apparently, the very technology that was giving voice to the masses was also, unfortunately, giving voice to the masses! Anyone and everyone with a computer microphone and an internet connection could claim the title of Host and add another pounding drum to the cacophony of pounding drums performing for the vast internet audience. Navigating this noise was as frustrating as it was fascinating.

Still, I wondered, would the phenomenon of the radio podcast open the doors for me to once again be a broadcaster? Would a TTA radio show fill a necessary niche, providing a polished and (hopefully) entertaining forum for atheist-related storytelling, discussion and debate? Would the atheist community respond to a former Christian in the host chair? Would I wind up merely talking to myself?

A few days after my guest slot on God Discussion, I registered The Thinking Atheist as a host on Blog Talk Radio, and in short order, I had scheduled my very first show for July 31st, 2010. It was titled, "What Christians Don't Know About Their Own Bible." I was nervous about doing a 90-minute, commercial-free solo run on my first outing, so I scheduled TTA's very first radio guest, AronRa, a popular atheist activist with a significant following and a solid reputation.

Despite my nervous fumbling and not-properly-calibrated (aka: distorted) audio, that first podcast jumped out of the gate with 762 live listeners and put the TTA broadcast vehicle in motion. The Thinking Atheist Radio Podcast was received with enthusiasm and goodwill and slid into (for the first year) a bi-weekly format with an international reach.

I wasn't a widely-recognized radio host. I didn't have a long list of impressive credentials. I was just a guy with a story doing the only thing he knew how to do. Perhaps it was that kind of accessible, unpretentious, even lackluster pedigree that audiences found ingratiating. Listeners seemed to enjoy my relaxed, rage-free style, and the quality production values seemed to help. Whatever the reasons for my success, people started dialing into the show on BlogTalkRadio, YouTube, iTunes, and other platforms, and the TTA podcast became popular.

During the entire month of August, 2010, The Thinking Atheist Podcast drew in 1,932 total listens. By January of the New Year within a mere five months of the show launch, that number had grown to over 35,000. January 2012 listens totaled 120,842 and began to grow exponentially.

And at the time of this Second Edition printing for "Deconverted," The Thinking Atheist Podcast – now hosted on Spreaker - has been downloaded over 50 million times worldwide.

Fifty million? Who are these people?

Well, they're people just like you and me. They're fathers, mothers, siblings, professionals, homemakers, students, teachers, young, old, affluent, underprivileged, out, closeted, bold, shy, apostates, lifelong atheists, white, black and every color of the rainbow. Every week, my switchboard is filled with the most amazing variety of people calling in from places domestic and foreign. Every week, we all come together to learn, share anecdotes, ask questions, vent, challenge each other, enjoy the company of friends, and remind each other that we're not alone.

As The Thinking Atheist podcast grows, I continue to examine future possibilities in the hopes that TTA can continue to thrive and expand, perhaps one day evolving into a larger, more visible and more influential entity. Some might bemoan the transition from this grassroots operation into a known quantity (much like the fan of an indie band might fear an eventual hit album), but I honestly feel like the conversations and discussions on our weekly show deserve the largest possible audience.

Certainly, I'd take pains to preserve the key elements that are making TTA radio successful, but if the circumstances were right, I could one day welcome the day when The Thinking Atheist Radio Podcast originates from an actual broadcast studio and sits on the radio dial right next to Family Life Radio and The 700 Club.

An atheist radio show peeking up over a herd of cozy, insulated and largely unchallenged religious programs? Now wouldn't THAT be a scandal!

"There is a difference between knowledge and belief, and I know which I prefer."

- **Peter / United Kingdom**

CHAPTER 19
Changing Minds (Even Our Own)

It's weird where the roads of life take us. My little world used to be relatively quiet. Just a few years ago, I was spoken of fondly by my mother and father. I had an intact first marriage. I participated in religious traditions and enjoyed Christian music. I maintained a position of good repute with pastors and church leaders. I gave very few people any cause to raise an eyebrow at me.

Today, I'm the guy religious people likely lament at prayer meetings. Three years into my TTA portfolio, highlights of my video work included.

- Depictions of a Sunday school teacher demonstrating the concept of Hell with a skull-embossed cigarette lighter and an aerosol can (VIDEO: "God is Good, But He is Also Just")

- Jesus miraculously appearing on a grilled cheese sandwich, a fish stick, and in the foam of a cappuccino (VIDEO: "It's a Miracle!")

- Eve in the Garden of Eden with bluebirds hiding her nipples (VIDEO: "The Story of Creation")

- David serving up a steaming plate of foreskins to King Saul (VIDEO: "Foreskin Follies")

- Christ rising from the grave to exact Rambo-style revenge on his executioners (VIDEO: "Jesus- The Revenge")

- A virile Noah in the honeymoon suite preparing to father three sons (VIDEO: "Noah's Ark – God, Giraffes & Genocide")

- A look at the condescending platitudes, like "I'll pray for you," doled out by the religious (VIDEO: "Understanding Christianese")

- A handy scriptural guide on how intensely Christians are allowed to flog the humans they own as property (VIDEO: "How To Beat Your Slave")

- Biblical instruction on when a woman's hand should be severed after touching the genital area of her spouse (VIDEO: "Hands Off!")

- An examination of how all religious contributions to society are trumped by even the most meager of scientific contributions, including water filters, GPS systems, memory foam and breast implants (VIDEO: "You Can't Trust Science.")

Ten years on, the temperature of my atheist activism has changed somewhat. It's still therapeutic to stir the bucket of blasphemy (demonstrating my own liberation from fear and religious control), but overall, the biting tone, the sarcasm, and the ridicule have given way to a more tempered, thoughtful, compassionate approach. I still believe that absurd ideas are candidates for mockery, but only on the larger stage where observers aren't challenged directly and can still feel a measure of safety. In other words, I don't use ridicule in my one-on-one conversations…only at the "macro" level with a broad audience.

These days, my personal interactions with believers often integrate the "Street Epistemology" approach, involving a lot of questions presented with sincerity and empathy. ("Epistemology" is the study of knowledge.) This Socratic Method has great utility, because it keeps the burdens of proof on those making Truth claims, and it challenges them to – perhaps for the first time in their lives – examine the reasons for cherished beliefs. Dr. Daniel Dennett has often spoken about religious belief in belief, and Street Epistemology cuts through any unconsidered faith claims in a search for the "why" and the "how." A few examples of questions asked.

- Why do you worship this specific god over the god of a different religion?

- How do you know the voice or sensation you're experiencing is God?

- If your religious belief is rooted in faith, do you embrace the faith claims for other gods equally?

- If a neutral observer heard Christian testimony next to an Islamic testimony, how could he/she know which one might be true?

- Do you believe in a literal Bible, Qur'an, etc? Why? If not literal, how do you determine which verses/stories to accept or ignore as literal?

YouTube has some great videos of Street Epistemology in action, and www.streetepistemology.com is a wonderful resource for those who, like me, realize that individual believers will likely never be ridiculed out of their cherished faiths. Rather, direct ridicule will make them feel personally attacked, they'll double down (and perhaps shut down), and both parties will march off in frustration.

This has been true in my own activism. I have never browbeaten a Christian into epiphany. My one-on-one successes have always come when I approached individual believers with goodwill, good humor, a listening ear, and empathy...refusing to devolve into conversation stoppers like, "You're wrong!" and "That's crazy!" (Imagine how you'd react if a debate opponent used this same language toward you.)

Insults and shouts are not effective tools for defeating bad ideas, and I'm increasingly convinced that we can (and should) re-humanize our interactions with interlocutors.

On a more personal note, I'm glad to have transitioned out of an angry apostasy. I realize that I had good reasons for anger. I'd been brainwashed into superstition. My legitimate doubts and questions were often blown back into my face by cultural Christians who couldn't even name the author of the Book of Genesis. I was genuinely aghast at the bigotry and privilege excused and enjoyed by American Christianity. And I had become part of a demographic so maligned as to be locked out of certain jobs, social connections, political activism, even family trust. Many atheists who experience this are understandably angry, and when the rejection of superstition makes you a second-class citizen, anger is a justifiable response, and it can be an effective motivator for change.

But there must be more to living than anger.

Back in 2009, I was agitated and exasperated. My early work was fueled by discontent, impatience, and constant annoyance. But those early years saw the fog of my exasperation begin to lift, and I realized the emotional (and physical) toll exacted by my own constant outrage. I had been burning my candle at both ends, and it did *not* give off a lovely light.

Having rejected any notions of an afterlife, I realized that I was cheating myself out of this life. I was spending so much time cursing the darkness that I wasn't sharing or enjoying any time in the sun. I not only needed to stop and smell the roses, but I needed to plant and cultivate some as well. There were experiences to have, places to see, people to love, goals to achieve, joys to be experienced far above the grinding gears of religious criticism.

I needed balance. I needed to start living again.

Interestingly, as I began to reconnect with my own humanity, I also began to have more success in my interactions with the religious. My life - rich with love and goodness - more resembled something they might want to explore or emulate. This – I think – speaks to a legitimate challenge that atheist activists have regarding human connection and community.

When we encourage believers to walk away from the church, we're not merely asking them to reject magical thinking. For them, church is the frame for the portrait of their lives. It's the welcome on Sunday mornings. It's where their kids make friends in Sunday School. It's the support group after a divorce, or through addiction recovery, or in times of emotional or financial crisis. It's the pool from which they draw their friendships. It's where they exchanged wedding vows or attended a grandmother's funeral. The church is their hub for gatherings, activities, concerts, inspirational words, and the reassurance that, despite life's many challenges, there is always a safe place to land.

Granted, the best parts of the church/community model are Humanistic, but the non-religious are playing catch-up in regard to providing these types of resources. If we're seeing the falling away of fresh apostates from their congregations, it's critical that these people have a safe place to land. For this reason (and because human beings are communal creatures by nature), community remains a real challenge for atheists/Humanists to meet. And we should do so.

We atheists can provide the friendship, the support, the resources for recovery and growth without any religious backstory, and as 23% of Americans now identify as non-religious[11], the need for community is greater than ever.

---

11   Scientific American: The Number of Americans with No Religious Affiliation Is Rising

"I find it very sad that people could reject their own flesh and blood for blind faith, and I've come to the realization that religion has truly imprisoned these peoples' minds."

- **Phil / British Columbia, Canada**

CHAPTER 20
Atheism Isn't a Worldview

I've mentioned the struggles and frustrations that come when dealing with religious claims and claimants. And again, those frustrations are valid.

Christian apologists teach impressionable children that the planet is younger than the Sumerian civilization. They allege that secular scientists (in league with Lucifer) have altered the geologic column to hide the evidence of Noah's flood. They assert that the tyrannosaurus rex, apparently vegetarian, happily romped in the Garden of Eden with Adam and Eve. They credit God for healing children treated (often at significant expense) by trained, human physicians. They claim the Ten Commandments as the ultimate moral code while being unable to name even half of them from memory. They claim divine protection as they lock their doors, click their seatbelts, carry their mace, wear their protective gear, and load their firearms. They betray the designs of the USA's own founding fathers by claiming that this nation belongs to Christianity. And they wail in protest when anyone disputes their "true" stories about the ancient superbaby conceived via ghost sex and born of a virgin for the purpose of blood magic to rescue humanity from a torture chamber that God, himself, created.

Yeah, battling religion can be maddening.

I also sometimes struggle with The Atheist Movement (and I'll come back to this label), as the years have seen no shortage of division, drama, and scandal within atheist circles. Many religious people are quick to point out our many issues and declare them a Devil Problem. Of course, any objective eye can see plenty of division, drama, and scandal within church circles, so if that claim was actually true, it would contradict Isaiah 54's promise that "no weapon that is formed against thee shall prosper." And we've already covered so many examples of malady and malice destroying the lives of the religious.

No, the public disagreements, the squabbling, the call-outs, the nasty Twitter wars, the splitting and splintering among atheist activists and organizations aren't linked to Satan. They're more accurately a reflection of human imperfection, sometimes misguided tactics embraced in the name of justice, and our evolved, tribalistic instincts. Tribes can be a beneficial thing, but in our hyper-divided world of the In-Group and Out-Group, tribes are too often cheating worthy causes out of legitimate allies. People differ, bicker, rally, divide, and vilify over issues both large and miniscule, fueling the fires of tribal division under a banner of ideological purity.

The religious are guilty of this. Atheists are guilty of this. And especially online, any casual observer might fear that atheists are as disunified as the thousands of religious denominations.

This is complicated, but let me try and explain.

Atheism is merely the rejection of a god belief. Atheism isn't a worldview, a political party, a dogma, or a set of requirements. Atheists come in all shapes and stripes, some wonderful, some awful, som Humanistic, some nihilistic, some rational, some delusional. If yo meet an atheist on the street, there's no guarantee that he/she came t atheism for rational reasons ("The aliens told me there is no God")

Just like in the church or any social group, we see humanity's bes worst, and the vast spectrum in-between. And this often translates t some very sticky interactions when opinions and personalities collide

There have been some very public clashes between some very pub lic atheists (I'll spare you the details; I want to stay focused on th bigger picture), and atheist activism has seen its share of scanda. Allegations of financial impropriety, professional dishonesty, eve sexual assault. Every year or two, there's a fresh headline tha prompts many to declare the whole of atheist activism tarnished an void, the bad apples effectively spoiling the entire barrel.

I completely disagree, for a few key reasons.

1. There is no "Atheist Movement." There's not any lone umbrel la organization which encapsulates and represents the whol of atheist activism. There are – in fact – many atheist move ments in a hugely diverse ecosystem of people and platforms American Atheists functions independently from the Secula Student Alliance, which functions separately from The Atheis Experience television show, which functions separately from the Atheist Republic website, which functions separately from hundreds of atheist YouTubers and audio podcasters, who func tion separately from authors and convention speakers, etc

   Declaring that atheist activism is any one thing is simply wrong headed, and when impropriety is rightly rooted out somewhere in the ether, this doesn't negate the desperate need for atheist/ Humanist activism in a world infected with superstition.

2. The fact that bad agents are sometimes exposed under the light of scrutiny reveals that good people are in fact working honorably to root out problems from within. As such, bad agency should be exposed, and the exposé should serve as a reminder that good people – while imperfect – are still fighting the good fight.

Beyond the biggest scandals, on a more personal level, I would like to see more concentrated attempts at understanding and unity among my fellow activists. Certainly, especially on Twitter, I've been guilty of my share of snark, but that sarcasm never seemed to change a mind, build a bridge, make a friend, or create an ally. The clever jabs are satisfying in the moment, but I'm aware that those comments are largely anti-discourse and usually only entrench my antagonists in their foxholes. For that reason (and I'm working on this), I'm trying to reserve my snarkiest comments for the obvious charlatans and religious/political con artists.

I watch with horror as online exchanges almost immediately devolve into ad hominems and insults. *You're wrong. You're stupid. You suck. You're garbage. Fuck you. No, fuck you!* It's so disheartening, and atheist activists (often operating from a perch of self-appointed intellectual superiority) can get caught up in these toxic exchanges as quickly as anyone. It doesn't mean they're bad people. It means that we're all navigating this relatively new social media world, and it's easy to forget that we're dealing with a person behind the two-dimensional avatar.

If you're a religious doubter or fresh apostate, please don't let the imperfection of other people keep you from continuing your own journey. If you see a public scrap over an atheism-related issue, or if you're told about a public activist shrouded in scandal, remember that these same problems exist within the church, within political parties, within any group involving human beings. Try to seek out the good people, and stay focused on the ideas beyond the idealogues.

I'll say the following with absolute conviction. Despite the many challenges, I would never take the Blue Pill and go back into the cocoon of my former religious life. My decade beyond the church walls has given me a perspective that satisfies in a way that Christianity never did. The places I've discovered, the people I've met, the things I've learned are priceless to me in a way that I can scarcely put into words.

It is my hope that the same can be true for you.

"A weight had been lifted from my chest. The absence of religion in my life has made me a more fulfilled, happier, and more peaceful human being."

-     **Trey / Denton, Texas**

CHAPTER 21
Ignorance is a Choice

In this final chapter, I wanted to address some of the questions and challenges posed to atheists by the religious and clarify why I feel the religious/atheist debate is a necessary, often beneficial thing. Perhaps the answers provided will assist you as you field these same questions in your own circle.

Why Can't You Just Leave Religion Alone?

The answer is simple. Atheist activism exists because religion exists.

Religion permeates our culture, shows up on our doorsteps with literature, scriptures, and threats of eternal damnation, influences our science books, contaminates our political systems, indoctrinates our children, and postulates that its doctrine must be followed, lest we be destroyed in body, in soul, or both. Non-believers are simply responding to the avalanche of religious messages that bears down upon us daily.

If the religious lived in a bubble where no ripple effects negatively impacted others, there would be no problem. But religion does not exist in a bubble. It accosts us in our homes, in our places of work, in our personal and professional lives. Believers are charged with a lifelong mission to preach, teach, disciple, shout it from the mountaintops, and to "go ye into all the world and preach the gospel to every creature." And when the skeptic raises a hand of protest, he is dismissed as misguided, immoral, rudderless, angry, or (wait for it) "religious about his atheism."

Is that a fair assessment? When's the last time an atheist rang your doorbell with brochures about the Good News of Humanism? How often do you find Richard Dawkins books in the dresser drawers of your hotel rooms? When was the last atheist temple erected in your neighborhood? Have you ever attended an atheist revival? Has atheism demanded 10% of your household income? How many dedicated atheist television channels broadcast through your satellite dish? How many atheist verses were you instructed to memorize as a child? When's the last time someone thanked a farmer (or even the cook) at the dinner table instead of God?

On a more radical front, what's the name of the last atheist who sawed the head off of an "infidel?" Or sentenced a shrouded woman to death for displeasing an oppressive husband? Or strapped explosives to his belt in order to kill hundreds in a public square? Or publicly hung a homosexual for being gay?

When atrocities carried out against our fellow human beings are rooted in religious ideology, we shouldn't – we can't – just leave religion alone. We must speak up and speak out.

Why Do You Hate God?

How can I hate something if I'm unconvinced that it exists.

Do You Think Religious People Are Stupid?

No. There are certainly stupid ideas and claims (study Scientolog sometime for a case study), but many intelligent people embrace religious faith. This doesn't validate the faith itself. It simply mean that the human brain is very modular, and people can quite deftl use rationality about Subject A without doing the same for Subjec B. At the end of the day, facts aren't measured by I.Q. points. Fact are determined through the scientific method. So let's look beyon the people to the evidence for and against any given Truth claim.

Don't All Belief Systems Deserve Respect?

People get respect, but ideas must earn it. Here in the 21st century, i someone declares that the earth is flat and expects his belief to be "re spected," he shouldn't be personally attacked, but he should prepar himself as his outlandish assertions are stacked, skewered, and roast ed over the white-hot flames of science, reason, and the evidence.

Isn't Atheism Just Another Religion?

No. Atheism is the lack of any God-belief. It has no deity, no dogma no worldview, no holy book, no posthumous existence...none of the attributes of a religion.

The declaration, "I'm unconvinced about your Truth claim" isn' itself a Truth claim.

What Do You Think Happens When You Die?

Brain function ceases. Consciousness ceases. The heat energy, elec trical energy, and chemical energy of the body are then assimilated into the environment as the body decays. It's as it was before you were born. If evidence for an afterlife (beyond unverifiable personal testimony) is ever found, I'm perfectly willing to change my mind.

Until then, I operate with the information I have, and that information strongly suggests a single, finite existence.

Don't You Find It Sad To Have No Afterlife?

It's strange, but I have actually found greater joy and purpose realizing that life is temporary, and that there may be no tomorrow. As such, I find greater urgency to maximize every moment, to say the right words, to demonstrate love and goodness, to set and achieve goals, to make memories, and to extract the marrow from every single day.

But If It's All Temporary, Why Bother Living?

A beloved piece of music has a final note. Is it not worth hearing? A delicious meal has a final bite. Is it not worth eating? A relaxing vacation has a final day. Is it not worth taking? A cherished friend has a final breath. Is that person not worth loving?

Why must something last forever to have value?

If You Don't Believe in God, Where Do You Find Purpose?

I can generate my own sense of purpose. I need not have it handed down by a third-party. Former pastor Dan Barker has a wonderful book on this subject titled, "Life Driven Purpose: How an Atheist Finds Meaning." I highly recommend it.

Atheists Believe in Nothing

As my paragraphs above revealed, a non-belief in gods doesn't also mean that atheists are empty shells. My Humanistic values don't require religion to be important, driving forces in my life, and I strongly believe in love, family, friendship, goodness for its own sake, integrity, honesty, compassion, and justice.

This atheist believes in a great many things.

But Where Do Your Morals Come From?

As we've determined earlier in this book, even if it was proven to be true, the Bible is a terrible source for someone's moral code. Ethical systems are actually easily explainable in the evolutionary model, as what helps another helps the species (which – in turn – helps the individual), and even altruistic actions benefit us from within and without.

Primatologist Frans de Waal has some wonderful research on primate social behaviors, emotional responses, cooperation, and morality. As an introduction to this subject, I also recommend a searchable online article by neuroscientist Sam Harris titled, "The Myth of Secular Moral Chaos."

What About The Evidence Proving Christianity? Like The Shroud of Turin?

The Shroud of Turin was an obvious fake. Radiocarbon dating reveals that the Shroud's linen is from the Mediaeval Period, more than 1,000 years after the supposed death of Christ.

But Carbon Dating Isn't Accurate!

Carbon dating IS accurate if you use it correctly. Radiocarbon dating works on objects up to 20,000 years old (which explains why you can't use this procedure on fossils). For older objects, there are dozens of other reliable methods of radiometric dating. DNA dating works up to 15,000 years. Paleomagnetic dating covers 250,000-1,000,000 years. Radiometric dating is effective 100,000 – 3.8 billion years.

The Second Law of Thermodynamics Proves Intelligent Design

The argument here is that evolved life wouldn't become more organized with time, but rather would spin into greater disorder over time. Apologists like to claim the Second Law as proof that biological systems couldn't see complex life evolving from simple cells, etc. This argument misunderstands (or misrepresents) the Second Law, which actually states that the total entropy – or gradual decline into disorder – cannot decrease in a closed system.

But our planet receives light and heat from the sun, and because it does, it is not a closed system. The solar fuel injects all kinds of possibilities for the organization and adaptation of life on earth.

Finally, if you want to discover just how much (or how little) the religious claimant knows about the subject, ask him what the other three Laws of Thermodynamics are and how they work

The Human Eye Is Too Complex To Have Evolved.

Actually, one can observe the various stages of evolved eyes even today, from the photosensitive sells of the euglena, to the pinhole eye of the nautilus, to the complex eye of the Antarctic Krill.

Charles Darwin himself spent pages discussing how the eye could have evolved:

..if numerous gradations from a perfect and complex eye to one very imperfect and simple, each grade being useful to its possessor, can be shown to exist; if further, the eye does vary ever so slightly, and the variations be inherited, which is certainly the case; and if any variation or modification in the organ be ever useful to an animal under changing conditions of life, then the difficulty of believing that a perfect and complex eye could be formed by natural selection, though insuperable by our imagination, can hardly be considered real." -Charles Darwin "On the Origin of Species" (1859).

Both Richard Dawkins and Sir David Attenborough have videos that provide a wonderful explanation of this for the non-scientist, identically titled "The Evolution of the Eye" and easily found on YouTube.

Side note: The next time a religious apologist mentions the eye as proof of an Intelligent Designer, check to see if he/she is wearing scientifically developed corrective lenses. That's called irony, folks.

There Are No Transitional Fossils.

Actually, scientists have discovered hundreds, perhaps thousands of examples, including the Tiktaalik (walking fish), Archaeopteryx (early birds), Ambulocetus (walking whale), and the Amphistium (early relative of the flatfish). Professor and paleontologist Donald R. Prothero's book, "Evolution: What the Fossils Say and Why it Matters" is a wonderful resource on the subject

Evolution Is Just A Theory.

A scientific theory is different than an untested idea, but is instead a scientifically accepted general principle supported by evidence and observed facts. Scientific theories are testable and make falsifiable predictions. As such, they can be both "theory" and "fact."

The Oxford English Dictionary defines a theory in this context as:

A scheme or system of ideas or statements held as an explanation or account of a group of facts or phenomena; a hypothesis that has been confirmed or established by observation or experiment, and is propounded or accepted as accounting for the known facts; a statement of what are held to be the general laws, principles or causes of something known or observed.

Examples are the Theory of Relativity, Game Theory, Heliocentrism, and the Theory of Gravity. This scientific type of theory is not the same as a hypothesis or guess. It is rooted in hard data and considered a reliable law.

Charles Darwin Converted To Christianity On His Death Bed.

No. Contrary to urban legend, Charles Darwin never had a death-bed conversion to Christianity at the leading of British evangelist Elizabeth "Lady" Hope, and his own children verify that he remained agnostic to the end.

Hitler Was An Atheist And "Evolutionist."

Hitler didn't endorse evolution. He practiced eugenics, which was an attempt to improve the quality of future generations by eliminating undesirable elements.

Evolution, unlike eugenics, benefits from a larger and more dynamic gene pool.

Hitler banned and/or burned Darwin's books. He also banned "all writings that ridicule, belittle or besmirch the Christian religion and its institution, faith in God."[12] He was raised Catholic and embraced Christianity. He had ties to the Catholic Church and invoked God in private and in public.

"My feelings as a Christian points me to my Lord and Savior as a fighter. It points me to the man who once in loneliness, surrounded by a few followers, recognized these Jews for what they were and summoned men to fight against them and who, God's truth! was greatest not as a sufferer but as a fighter. In boundless love as a Christian and as a man I read through the passage which tells us how the Lord at last rose in His might and seized the scourge to drive out of the Temple the brood of vipers and adders. How terrific was His fight for the world against the Jewish poison. To-day after two thousand years, with deepest emotion I recognize more profoundly than ever before the fact that it was for this that He had to shed His blood upon the Cross. As a Christian I have no duty to allow myself to be cheated, but I have the duty to be a fighter for truth and justice... And if there is anything which could demonstrate that we are acting rightly it is the distress that daily grows For as a Christian I have also a duty to my own people."[13] – Adolf Hitler

Nazi SS uniforms even saw belt buckles bearing the words "GOTT MIT UNS," translated "GOD WITH US." Indeed, the murderer, tyrant believed he was doing God's good work.

---

12 Leonidas Hill "The Nazi Attack on Un-German Literature 1933-1945"
13 Adolf Hitler, April 12, 1922 / Norman Baynes, "The Speeches of Adolf Hitler"

Albert Einstein Was A Christian.

Incorrect. Consider the words of Einstein himself.

"It was, of course, a lie what you read about my religious convictions, a lie which is being systematically repeated. I do not believe in a personal God and I have never denied this but have expressed it clearly. If something is in me which can be called religious then it is the unbounded admiration for the structure of the world so far as our science can reveal it." – Albert Einstein [14]

America Was Founded As A Christian Nation.

It was not. Nor were the founding fathers all religious. George Washington never declared himself a Christian. Thomas Paine rejected religion outright. James Madison spoke about "religious bondage" and how it "shackles and debilitates the mind." Benjamin Franklin and Thomas Jefferson were, at best, deists, with little or no allegiance to the Christian god.

There is no mention of God in the U.S. Constitution, and the mention of religion in the First Amendment serves to separate church and state:

Congress shall make no law respecting an establishment of religion, or prohibiting the free exercise thereof;

"In God We Trust" didn't appear on U.S. coins until the time of the Civil War, and it wasn't printed on paper currency until 1957. The words "under God" weren't part of the original U.S. Pledge of Allegiance, but were instead added by Congress in 1954.

---

14   March 24, 1954, from "Albert Einstein: The Human Side," Princeton University Press 1981 p. 43

The American founding fathers set up a government separate from any religion, clearly stated in Article 11 of the Treaty of Tripoli signed by John Adams in 1797: *"The Government of the United States of America is not, in any sense, founded on the Christian religion."*

Constitutional attorney Andrew Seidel's book "The Founding Myth: Why Christian Nationalism Is Un-American" is a comprehensive resource on the Christian Nation claim.

I'd Rather Believe In God And Be Wrong.

This assertion, also known as Pascal's Wager, betrays two revealing elements. One, the "just in case" position isn't true belief but merely an outward *masquerade* of true belief, and two, you just admitted that an omniscient god couldn't tell the difference.

There Are No Atheists In Foxholes.

Tell that to the family of Pat Tillman, an NFL player who served in the United States Army in the wake of the September 11th attacks. He was killed by friendly fire in April of 2004, and his story was produced into a 2010 documentary film, "The Tillman Story." Pat Tillman served his country with honor. And he was an outspoken atheist.

According to a 2015 article in Christianity Today, the Department of Defense's statistics on religion has more atheists than Southern Baptists in the U.S. Military[15], the Military Association of Atheists and Freethinkers reveals that the number of serving atheists nearly tripled from 2009 to 2017, and "No Religious Preference" (not necessarily atheist, but certainly not committed to a specific religion) is the single largest demographic in the armed forces at almost 23%.

---

15   Christianity Today "Atheists Outnumber Southern Baptists in US Military" 4-23-2015

Author and psychiatrist Dr. Andy Thompson has perhaps the best perspective on the claim that there are no atheists in foxholes:

"Maybe there are only atheists in foxholes. If the faithful truly and fully believe in a protective deity, why would they dive into a foxhole to protect themselves from the bullets whizzing by? A part of their brand knows damn well that if they do not protect themselves, the bullets will hardly discriminate between those who claim faith and those who reject it." - Dr. Andy Thompson, author of "Why We Believe in Gods"

Atheists Think The Universe Came From Nothing.

Well, again, atheism is merely the non-belief in gods. Atheism doesn't make any declarative statements about the origins of Life, the Universe, and Everything…beyond the rejection of supernatural explanations. Any claims of a god or Intelligent Designer bear the burden of proof. That said, I have yet to meet any atheist who spoke in the language of this popular religious meme:

ATHEISM

The belief that there was nothing and nothing happened to nothing and then nothing magically exploded for no reason, creating everything and then a bunch of everything magically rearranged itself for no reason whatsoever into self-replicating bits which then turned into dinosaurs.

Makes perfect sense.

This kind of anti-science rhetoric is designed as a conversation-stopper. It bandies the word "nothing" in ways designed to make atheism (and the acceptance of evolutionary science) sound ridiculous. At the same time, Christian apologists are saying it's more reasonable to accept that a cosmic wizard conjured hundreds of billions of galaxies so that a dirt-man and rib-woman could be created on a single planet within them.

These conversations deserve better than fill-in-the-blank supernatural answers. If someone wishes to fill the gaps in human understanding with "God did it," they're much like our primitive ancestors who believed that natural disasters were the products of divine wrath, that mental illness was an infestation of evil spirits, and that the earth (and its human passengers) were the center of the universe.

But Our Complex World Is Obviously, Intelligently Designed.

It's important to note that, from an engineering standpoint, the best designs aren't necessarily the most complex. In fact, the best designs are usually pared down to the simplest scenarios. As such, complexity might seem overwhelming to the human brain, but under the intense stress tests of biological science, it makes much more sense rooted in evolutionary explanations over religious ones.

The usual examples given for Intelligent Design are quickly revealed as problematic. The complex eye is covered above, as is the "transitional fossils" argument. Abiogenesis (or "life from non-living matter") isn't a religious question, and the fact that it's an unsolved mystery isn't any kind of proof for God. The claim that beneficial mutations are impossible without design is demonstrably false. Declarations that the Cambrian Explosion was a burst of designed biological diversity ignore the fact that the diversification took place over the span of over 20 million years. The list goes on.

Beyond that, anyone holding to an Intelligent Design belief must take into account so many examples of nonsensical or terrible design. Blind creatures with eyes. Deaf creatures with ears. Flightless birds with wings. Pelvises in legless animals. Cetaceans without gills. Two-thirds of the planet's surface uninhabitable by humans. A sun that gives us cancer. Tsunamis that kill hundreds of thousands in a single day. Human embryonic tails. Birth defects. Approximately half of human pregnancies resulting in miscarriage. Redundant DNA. Vestigial organs. Wisdom teeth. Degenerating eyesight. The extinction of 99% of all life that has ever existed on earth. And so many other examples.

Why would an Intelligent Designer create such a poor, often painful, and certainly wasteful design?

If Humans Came From Monkeys, Why Are There Still Monkeys?

There are some clever responses to this question. My favorites include, "If Americans came from Britain, why is there still Britain?" and "If the biblical Adam was created from dirt, why is there still dirt?"

Humans didn't actually come from monkeys. Humans and monkeys diverged from a common ancestor approximately seven million years ago. And as much as the church doesn't want to admit it, there's barely a 1% difference genetically between modern humans and chimpanzees.

The "Why are there still monkeys?" question is rooted in ignorance of evolution and a palpable fear many feel when they are informed that they are – in fact – higher primates…the human animal, and not the divinely-selected and eternally adopted child of a cosmic King

Ignore The Old Testament. Read The New Testament.

Christ himself affirmed and reinforced Old Testament law i
Matthew 5:17, ""Do not think that I have come to abolish the La
or the Prophets; I have not come to abolish them but to fulfill them.

Also, the rejection of the Old Testament would require that yo
also reject the human origin story of Adam and Eve, the glob
flood in Genesis 6, the stories of Joshua and Esther and Samson
and even the Ten Commandments. After all…they're located i
the Old Testament.

This meager list of challenges is obviously just a drop in the va
ocean of debate, but the above arguments are heard so loudly an
so often, I felt they warranted attention. I encourage you to go muc
deeper into these subjects, and www.thethinkingatheist.com pro
vides links to various websites, books, videos, and articles that cove
everything from Intelligent Design to religious history to evolutio
to critical dissections of the biblical Jesus story.

But why is this understanding so important? Why do non-believer
have to ruffle features, stir the pot, create unrest and cause so muc
trouble? Why do we fight this fight against religion's influence.

A perfect illustration for the necessity of critical thinking is dem
onstrated by my recent tour of the Creation Museum in Petersburg
Kentucky, a slick-as-Hollywood walkthrough of humankind'

origins per the Bible. The facility is a monument to bad science, bad history, and the gross indoctrination of children.

Founded by Ken Ham of Answers in Genesis, the Creation Museum asserts (with a straight face) that dinosaurs romped the Garden of Eden as unthreatening, vegetarian companions of Adam and Eve, that fang-bearing animals turned carnivorous only after Original Sin, that incest was God's method for repopulating the planet after the Great Flood, that the Grand Canyon was created in a few brief days as a product of that flood, and ultimately, that human reason (Man's Word) stands inferior to biblical Truth (God's Word) and is responsible for everything from gang violence to tornadoes to the attacks of 9/11.

As I took the tour, all around me were children-young, impressionable, eager, enthusiastic, vulnerable children-brought by religious families and private schools to experience God's plan in all of its glory. You can probably imagine these fresh faces gazing into the scale model of Noah's ark as dinosaurs, two by two, walked the boarding ramp before the first rains fell.

The Creation Museum hooks these kids by populating the first 10 minutes of the tour almost exclusively with dinosaurs. (I submit that the facility should be renamed, "Jurassic Lark.") Of course, once the child's senses are engaged, the tour kicks into full-bore indoctrination mode, asserting that humankind originated in a garden populated simultaneously with (no kidding) squirrels, penguins, and velociraptors. One scene actually shows a giggling Eve mere feet from a plant-eating raptor uninterested in her presence.

A few paces later, after an ominous representation of the Fall of Man, the exhibit turns dark, shrouding the child (and the parents) in messages about the unreliability of human intelligence and the perversion of human morality. It's a shame trip, informing all ticket holders that they are diseased while simultaneously selling them the cure.

In the Age of Information, I find it offensive that places like the Creation Museum exist. In fact, I find it offensive that the word "museum" is even part of the exhibit's title, as the 90-minute experience spits in the face of legitimate paleontology, archeology, cosmology, and history. It's a house of lies told with a straight face, and the visitors (at $29.95 per adult ticket) are being conditioned to build their worldviews upon Ken Ham's Guilt Emporium.

Religious children are being taught *what* to think. They should be taught *how* to think. Yet the Creation Museum's tactics of indoctrination exist as microcosm in religious homes and communities across the planet. Ignorance is celebrated. Curiosity is quelled. Fear is cultivated. Science is largely distrusted. And brainwashed individuals struggle to make sense of their own lives as they frantically struggle to pound the square peg of religion into the round hole of reason.

I understand that religion can give hope and comfort. Religion can be a very real coping mechanism in this tumultuous world, calming the grieving, selling purpose to the rudderless, bringing joy to the desperate. I've been to countless church services filled with hundreds (sometimes thousands) of ebullient men, women, and youth joined together in the singing, swaying, smiling, affirming, and motivating Sunday services, each attendee feeling a sense of empowerment and personal fulfillment, each emboldened that they are a commissioned soldier on a divine mission.

I've witnessed the good deeds done in God's name. Every day churches feed the hungry, build houses for the homeless, encourage the heartbroken, bring medicine for the sick, and so much more. And while history reveals a host of heinous deeds done in the name of religion, there's no denying that many religious entities commit good deeds in the name of their deity.

Unfortunately, with each good deed done in God's name comes the larger agenda: to create converts.

Missionaries traveling to impoverished countries often genuinely wish to build shelters and provide medicine, but their ultimate goal isn't the salvation of the material body. They've come for the soul. Churches involved in community outreach are advertising to the unchurched in an attempt to "grow" attendance and bring fresh souls into eternity. Each dollar spent, each mouth fed, each wound treated, each structure built is part of a marketing strategy to win hearts and minds. Religion is the smiling, clean-cut, baby-kissing politician that doles out utopian promises to win the election. And to borrow from Christopher Hitchens, there isn't a single moral action performed by a religious person that cannot be done with equal effectiveness by a non-believer. After all of the religious praying, naming, and claiming, at the end of the day, all benefits provided to the needy, hungry, and hurting are the products of human hands. Real solutions are 100% deity-free.

Religion would be innocuous enough if it existed in an incubator. Unfortunately, it doesn't. Religion casts its stones into the waters in the hopes of making the largest possible ripple. It pounds on the doors of our homes with religious tracts and warnings about Hell. It frightens children with tales of demons and fiery torture. It inhibits curiosity and encourages a slave mentality. It impedes real science. It contaminates a government designed by our founding fathers to be secular. It condemns good, moral, precious human beings for not fitting into the narrow cookie cutter of biblical sexuality. Its holy books promote slavery, racism, misogyny, and genocide. And it strives to deny to others the respect and freedom that it constantly demands for itself.

Personally, I'm weary of watching religious people play victim. They often exist in a perpetually pouty state of indignation, aghast that anyone would approach their supernatural claims with doubt or skepticism. They wail and protest, fingers planted firmly in their ears when challenged, and crying "Why are you stealing my joy?" when they are asked to prove the magical claims they're presenting as hard facts.

The burden of proof remains on those making the assertions, and if I may borrow from Christopher Hitchens again, "What can be asserted without evidence can be dismissed without evidence." I also love the forever quotable Robert Green Ingersoll's line from Orthodoxy: "The more false we destroy, the more room we make for the true."

Religion is the slammed door that keeps humankind from entering and enjoying this incredible age of discovery. It must be dismantled or broken through. And if discarding the superstitions of our primitive ancestors means that we'll be made (or we will make others) uncomfortable, should that discomfort be a barrier that prevents us from embracing reality?

This is a wonderful time to be alive. We're more equipped to examine our bodies, our minds, our origins, our planet, and the cosmos than any generation in history.

Think about it. Just a few decades ago, getting information often meant running an obstacle course for each and every answer to each nd every question. You could certainly find what you needed if ou had hours or days and lots of patience. But science books, his-ory books, peer-reviews, medical journals, and the lion's share of esearch-related information were often difficult to find and retrieve.

'resentations from our planet's greatest minds used to remain most-y hidden inside universities and lecture halls. Now, thanks to the ;ame-changing technology of the internet, the whole world is the ecture hall, and we're all invited to attend.

nformation, education, answers, discussion, debate, documentation, oft theories, and hard evidence are just a few keystrokes and a few minutes (or seconds) away. Sure, there are different planes of knowl-:dge and understanding, many of which are the domain of the expert, he career scientist, the Ph.D. But those of us outside those areas of :xpertise are no longer excluded from the discussion. We have the op-ortunity to learn and participate in ways never before possible.

We don't have an excuse for not doing our homework. For dig-;ing deeper. For checking facts and figures. For pursuing genu-ne understanding.

saw a poster recently which summed it up perfectly: *In the age of nformation, ignorance is a choice.*

Now, more than when I was a believer, I look up and around at the universe and truly feel a sense of awe. It's not some cheap, bum-per-sticker, feel-good "look at the pretty sunset" kind of awe. It's a genuine understanding that I'm a tiny speck living on a tiny speck inside a vast universe, but I'm alive, and I'm tremendously fortunate to draw breath during a period of fantastic invention and discovery.

I'm alive in a time where, every day, humans transport themselves to faraway destinations via flying machines traveling hundreds of times faster than a human can walk. We predict storms days before they occur. We drive to unfamiliar destinations as GPS systems guide us through every turn. Our TV remotes, our power tools. and our telephones have no cords. We can emulate an entire orchestra artificially with a single instrument. We put tracking devices in our pets so we can find them with satellites. We're touching the bottom of our deepest oceans. We cook our meals with one touch. We prevent pregnancy with one pill. We pay our bills with one click. We experience movies in three dimensions. We're using stem cells to dramatically change the treatment of disease. We're snapping photographs from the surface of Mars and sharing them here on planet earth. And who knows what the coming years will bring.

Instead of clutching onto the ham-handed explanations, doctrines, solutions, and instructions of ancestors who were essentially feeling their way in the dark, it's time to embrace the more satisfactory evidence that science provides, and be grateful that we're alive to see in action the microscope, the telescope, the video camera, the vaccine, the computer, the laser, the x-ray, the spacecraft, and so much more.

During this generation's intellectual growing pains, many will resist. They'll lament the rejection of superstitious notions. They'll look to the sky and continue to cry out to the deity, the ghost, the invisible friend. They'll fear a world that operates by natural laws instead of spiritual ones. For a host of rationalizations, they'll hold their sacred ground while humankind presses forward.

In my own life, I've discovered more satisfaction and joy in my godlessness than I ever did as a Christian. I commit kind and moral acts because I choose to, not because I seek heavenly reward. I acknowledge that my actions have consequences that I alone must bear responsibility for. I no longer carry anticipation of Heaven or fear of Hell. I've come to embrace curiosity and welcome doubt. I have fallen in love with science. And I have arrived at midlife with a firm conviction that, for it to truly achieve its potential, humankind must put to rest the antiquated, the outdated, the flawed, and the false assertions of its infancy.

It has been a long, difficult, heartbreaking, exhilarating, enlightening, and awe-inspiring journey. I don't know how The Thinking Atheist community will evolve in the years ahead, but I'm tremendously grateful to be a part of it, to see it grow, and to witness firsthand the support and encouragement it has given to others. Sure, it's never easy swimming against the religious tide, but "easy" is no longer my criteria for living. I'd rather life a difficult life truthfully than accept a lazy fantasy, and despite the challenges, I have found this evidence-based philosophy for living satisfying, empowering, and liberating.

The fog of superstitious thinking has lifted, and I have a breathtaking view of a better world.

CPSIA information can be obtained
at www.ICGtesting.com
Printed in the USA
LVHW111727040919
629921LV00009B/237/P